THE DEATH OF CHRISTIAN CULTURE

JOHN SENIOR

ARLINGTON HOUSE·PUBLISHERS
NEW ROCHELLE, NEW YORK

P 10 9 8 7 6 5 4 3 2 1

Book design by Pat Slesarchik

Manufactured in the United States of America

Senior, John, 1923–
    The death of Christian culture.

    Includes index.
    1. Civilization, Christian.   2. Christianity—20th century.
I. Title.
BR115.C5S46   261.5   78-16154
ISBN 0-87000-416-6

Uxori carissimae

Contents

1 What Is Christian Culture?

I

Matthew Arnold was one of the hinges on which the English-speaking world, a century ago, turned from Christianity to Modernism. He was a most fair-minded and articulate exponent of the Liberal view and, like many Liberals today, still thought of himself — somehow — as a Christian. But he wrote:

> In spite of the crimes and follies in which it lost itself, the French Revolution derives from the force, truth, and universality of the ideas which it took for its law, and from the passion with which it could inspire a multitude for these ideas, a unique and still living power; it is — it will probably long remain — the greatest, the most animating event in history.

Arnold had absorbed a classical education from a famous Christian father. He had the highest respect for Christianity, but did not believe it. The Revolution was the "greatest, the most animating event in history," he said — not the Crucifixion. He was convinced that the revolutionaries had carried things too far; but, make no mistake about it, he thought they had carried things too far in the right direction. The "religious problem," as he calls it, is how to reconceive Christianity so as to put it in the service of the Revolution.

> A fresh synthesis of the New Testament data — not a making war on them, in Voltaire's fashion, not leaving them out of mind, in the world's fashion, but the putting a new construction upon them, the taking them from under the old, traditional, conventional point of view and plac-

ing them under a new one — is the very essence of the
religious problem, as now presented and only by efforts in
this direction can it receive a solution.

The identification of the traditional with the conventional is, of
course, as old as sophistry and often serves as an opening for change.

But Christ Himself said, "Omnia mihi tradita sunt a Patre meo."
Christian doctrine is not the result of convention, though it is indeed
traditional: "All things have been handed down to me by the
Father." Christianity can never serve the times. According to the
Declaration of the Rights of Man, liberty is the power of doing what
we will, so long as it does not injure another. In a sense this can be true
(provided that the will is rightly formed). But according to the Liberal
view, "Do what thou wilt" includes willing to do what thou shouldst
not. The Liberal takes a stand in No Man's Land between "the law in
my members" and "the law in my mind." In that precarious and
self-righteous place, doing what thou wilt must always injure others,
if what thou wilt is separate from the good. By doing evil to others or
to ourselves, we first of all injure ourselves, because to do evil is the
worst thing that can happen to a man. And because we are members
of the human race, we injure the species even by an act only directed
against ourselves. If others consent, the harm reciprocally injures
everyone. There is no such thing as a victimless crime any more than a
free lunch. There is no such thing as a Christianity in which the
commandments of God are accommodated to the Rights of Man.

But to save appearances and secure a useful social continuity, the
Liberal thinks "religion" must be saved — though in the service of the
revolution and its new culture in which God will depend for His
existence on us. "Religion," Arnold writes,

> is the greatest and most important of the efforts by which
> the human race has manifested its impulses to perfect
> itself.

But no contingent being in itself can be the source of its own perfection, nor, given an infinity of contingent beings each dependent on
another, could they all together be a source of their own perfection.
Rather, some Being must exist necessarily, if any does contingently.
For Arnold, that order is reversed. The necessary is made dependent
on the contingent. And religion is

2

that voice of the deepest human experience, [which] does not only enjoin and sanction the aim which is the great aim of culture, the aim of setting ourselves to ascertain what perfection is and to make it prevail; but also, in determining generally in what perfection consists, religion comes to a conclusion identical with that of . . . culture.

For Arnold, religion works along with art, science, and philosophy to achieve what he calls "perfection." Perfection he defines in defiance of etymology:

It is in making endless additions to itself, in the endless expansion of its powers, in endless growth in wisdom and by beauty, that the spirit of the human race finds its ideal. To reach this ideal, culture is an indispensable aid, and that is the true value of culture. Not a having and a lasting, but a growing and a becoming is the character of perfection.

I said "in defiance of etymology" because the root of the word *perfection*, exactly opposite to "becoming," means "done," "complete," totally at rest, "having become" — *per-facere*. "To reach the ideal. . .," Arnold says. But how can an ideal of "endless growth" be reached? Here we have an old sophism dressed up as a new principle of Liberal religion — that perfection is becoming. The present historical task — always the present historical task in every age — is revolution, though Arnold more subtly insists that the revolution is best achieved by reinterpreting rather than simply destroying the past. At the metaphysical root of this error is the Heraclitean failure to solve the problem of the one and the many. Because nothing ever is, they say, there is nothing constant, only endless flux.

From this false view of becoming it immediately follows, and Arnold puts it in the same paragraph, that Liberal culture must be collectivist. For in an endless and contradictory movement there is no permanent substance. A person is a meaningless nonentity; so a number of coagulated nonentities, by their own collective contingency, must somehow create their being out in front of them. It is a kind of Indian rope trick in which a tissue of nonentities throws its finality into the air and climbs after it. This is the basis for religious

3

evolutionism — often confused with Newman's exactly contrary view of the development of doctrine — in which the whole of creation is forever hoisted on its own petard. Evolution, Newman insists, is not development. In development, what is given once and for all in the beginning is merely made explicit. What was given once and for all in Scripture and Tradition has been clarified in succeeding generations, but only by addition, never contradiction; whereas evolution proceeds by negation. Newman devotes a whole chapter in *An Essay on the Development of Christian Doctrine* to refuting the idea that anything contrary to dogma can ever be a proper development, nor anything not found in the consensus of the Fathers dogma. Put positively, development is radically conservative, permitting only that change which helps doctrine to remain *true* by defining errors that arise in every age against it. Doctrine grows, as Ronald Knox put it in a homely figure, like a horse's hoof, from trodding on hard, uneven ground.

The best of us are prone to sophistry when an obvious truth contradicts a strong desire. Recent ecumenical commissions from various churches have tried to create approaches to unity by reconstructing their articles of faith so as to make room for contradictory articles of faith held by others. Protestants and Catholics can both keep and give up their identities at the same time. Jacques Maritain, for example, speaking of a declaration of the Council of Florence notoriously obnoxious to any convergence of doctrine,* says:

> What matters here is the declaration itself, not the manner in which one understood it in that epoch . . . according to the mentality of the epoch, without having been conscious of the ambiguity . . . . It is with time that the ambiguity in question appeared — and at the same stroke the true sense in which the declaration must be taken. There has therefore been a mutation, not with regard to the declaration itself, but with regard to the manner in which those who formulated it understood it. The declaration is infallibly true (provided it is rightly understood).

Nemo potest extra ecclesiam salvus esse: "Salvation is impossible outside the Church."

Surely no Protestant in his right mind will accept an argument like this as the price of peace, because the whole Christian revelation, church authority, all authority, the noble mind of Maritain, and reason itself are here overthrown. "Words," said the Mad Hatter to Alice, "mean exactly whatever I say they mean." Go back to start! Begin again. We are here at the first of the first principles. A definition that includes its contradictory is not a definition at all. And any agreed statement by theologians who think this way is a trap. You will be signing a contract with a huckster who tomorrow will not be held to the bargain he struck according to his mentality of today. Peace at the price of one's reason can only be that "evil peace" St. Augustine speaks of as the violent enforcement of injustice. No. It is very much in the interest of everyone that clear distinctions be kept. The current defection of Catholic theologians from their own explicit doctrines is the worst setback for Protestants since they took up the puerilities of the Higher Criticism. If we are to love one another as ourselves, it is one another we must love, not ourselves pretending to be others, all the while pretending others to be ourselves. It is easy for men of good will (and bad will) to come together if they affirm contradictions. "The declaration is infallibly true (provided it is rightly understood)." That is either a truism — anything must be rightly understood — or what used to be called "jesuitical." Understood by whom? Gospels, Epistles, the Law and the Prophets, creeds, confessions — all these are infallibly true if "rightly understood" according to the ideals of the French Revolution and the mind of Maritain, and the mind of the mind that understands the mind of Maritain . . . . *Infallible?* Such music hath a dying *fall.* The only rational way for Protestants and Catholics to get along together is to practice the difficult virtue of tolerance — not to falsify their claims by ambiguities.

"A fresh synthesis of the New Testament data," Arnold urged. "Not a making war on them, in Voltaire's fashion, not leaving them out of mind in the world's fashion, but the putting a new construction on them." Frankly, I prefer Voltaire; the fox to the weasel; the wolf in sheep's to the wolf in shepherd's clothing.

Arnold explains how this reconstruction of the New Testament data must involve a collectivity.

> The expansion of our humanity to suit the idea of perfection which culture forms, must be a *general* expansion.

Perfection as culture conceives it, is not possible while the individual remains isolated. The individual is required under pain of being stunted and enfeebled in his own development if he disobeys, to carry others along with him in his march toward perfection, to be continually doing all he can to enlarge and increase the volume of the human stream sweeping thitherward. And here once more, culture lays on us the same obligation as religion, which says, as Bishop Wilson has admirably put it, that "to promote the kingdom of God is to increase and hasten one's own happiness."

There he goes, putting a new construction on the plain meaning of words: surely the Bishop did not think that the kingdom of God is culture. For the Christian, to promote the kingdom of God increases one's happiness because in loving our neighbor as ourselves we increase our own love of God, which is a participation in eternal life. It has nothing at all to do with perfection of the secular city. Arnold has identified the kingdom of God with the Benthamite idea of the greatest good for the greatest number. He has repeated the folly of Auguste Comte who, as Christopher Dawson put it, believed that humanity was a reality while the individual person was an abstraction. Note how often he uses abstractions as personal agents: "As culture conceives it . . . culture lays on us the obligation . . ." Arnold is not interpreting Christian doctrine but parading an old collective hedonism in new clothes. The "religious problem" for Christians has always been the same: to love God with all our heart, soul, mind, and strength and our neighbor as ourself.

What the Modernist means by "mentality" or the "mentality of the epoch" is the imagination, which gives a kind of halfway knowledge of material objects. An image, to the extent that it exists, exists in the mind, so that a reality outside the mind is spiritualized, retaining, however, the accidents of its concrete existence, its outward qualities — quantity, shape, color, and so on. When the imagination is taken as the terminus of mind and used to judge the meaning of doctrine, concepts are reduced to images: what we wish can seem to be what is. Thus, in the first kind of error that the imagination may commit, the mind simply does not "see" the concept — naturally, because concepts are invisible — and refuses therefore to acknowledge its existence. In the second kind of error, the image takes the place of the concept and we get that reaction called "Epiphany" by Joyce — "God is a shout in the street" — so that theology and philosophy become poetry, and reason metaphor. Philosophical and religious "systems" are enjoyed as if they were works of art; we may prefer Christianity or Buddhism, admiring both, or Plato's or Spinoza's metaphysics.

Unless the mind achieves its perfection in the making of conceptual judgments, religion and philosophy cannot be understood; and with religion and philosophy gone, all human activity is rudderless.

Surrounded as we are by a hedonistic and even demonic imaginative ground, it is not impossible, of course, but very difficult for the intellect to grasp ideas like "spirit," "soul," "God." We are doubly blocked: to restore the imagination, we must put the intellect in its proper place; but to put the intellect first, we must have restored the imagination.

The direct study of philosophy and theology will not cure a diseased imagination, because anyone with a diseased imagination is incapable of studying philosophy and theology. Popularizations like Gilson's and Maritain's, though salutary, are insufficient. They started a Neoscholastic fad that like the others of the day flourished, faded, and is gone, because the proper study of these subjects presupposes an immersion in Christian culture. Despite a lifetime study of St. Thomas, Maritain himself, blinded by desire, fell into the same errors he had refuted in others.

What is so appalling about the new theologians — even Maritain — is not only the theology but the kitsch. They celebrate surrealistic poetry and art. They seem actually to believe that Christianity can be "updated" by translating its concepts into alien and shoddy literary stuff — into music measured only by decibels of noise. The word "culture," as they use it, is indeed ambiguous: in the strict sense there is only one culture, that of the Christian, Latin West. In another, as used by anthropologists, it means any *milieu* — and thus we may speak of a Bantu or even a British "culture." The only way to bring Christianity to the Bantu or the British, however, is to bring them clothes, chairs, bread, wine, and Latin. Belloc was exactly right in his famous epigram: "The Faith is Europe, Europe is the Faith." The deep foundation of English Protestant and even neopagan poetry is the Latin Mass and Benedictine Office. If we want to bring Christianity to other cultures in the anthropological sense, we must first restore the real culture of Christendom in ourselves. Too often we have exported an empty missionary cant along with economic capital. Christ was born in the fullness of time into a definite place. Classical culture was and is the *praeparatio fidei*, its philosophy and literature the Egyptian gold and silver Christendom has taken on its pilgrimage. The Church has grown in a particular way and has always brought its habits with it, so that wherever it has gone it has been a European thing — stretched, adapted, but essentially a European thing.

The beginning of the cure of a sick theology, for English-speaking people, is a schoolboy course in Chaucer, Shakespeare, Milton, and even Matthew Arnold, in the disciplined sounds of honest, English music —

> Such Musick (as 'tis said)
> Before was never made,
>   But when of old the sons of morning sung,
> While the Creator great
> His constellations set,
>   And the well-ballanc't world on hinges hung,
> And cast the dark foundations deep,
> And bid the weltring waves their oozy channel keep.

II

Culture, as in "agriculture," is the cultivation of the soil from which men grow. To determine proper methods, we must have a clear idea of the crop. "What is man?" the Penny Catechism asks, and answers: "A creature made in the image and likeness of God, to know, love and serve Him." Culture, therefore, clearly has this simple end, no matter how complex or difficult the means. Our happiness consists in a perfection that is no mere endless hedonistic whoosh through space and time, but the achievement of that definite love and knowledge which is final and complete. All the paraphernalia of our lives, intellectual, moral, social, psychological, and physical, has this end: Christian culture is the cultivation of saints.

There have been many "cultures" in the other sense since the Fall, many attempts to establish a new Eden for man. Most of them have been ruled by demons under

> . . . their great Dictator, whose attempt
> At first against mánkind so well had thriv'd
> In Adam's overthrow, and led their march
> From Hell's deep-vaulted Den to dwell in light,
> Regents and Potentates, and Kings, *yea gods*
> Of many a pleasant Realm and province wide.

It was a sorry thing to read in the papers of a Benedictine mission-ary in India who censured St. Francis Xavier for having said that Hindu gods were devils, an attitude the monk found "medieval," which indeed it is, but then it is Baroque, Neoclassic, and Romantic as well, and universally Christian, as the Psalms and *Paradise Lost* attest:

> For all the gods of the Gentiles are devils (Psalm 95:6),

and

> Through God's high sufferance for the trial of man,
> By falsities and lyes the greatest part
> Of Mankind they corrupted to forsake
> God their Creator, and th' invisible
> Glory of him that made them, to transform
> Oft to the Image of a Brute, adorn'd
> With gay Religions full of Pomp and Gold,
> And Devils to adore for Deities.

Thus Milton starts his horrid catalogue at Satan's great Consult in Pandaemonium, beginning with Moloch and the fiends named in the Old Testament, then proceeding to less malicious ones all the cold and airy way to Mount Olympus. The Greek Ideal too, although it prepared us for the Faith despite itself — the Devil being of God's party without knowing it — is demonic in inspiration. Socrates was guided by a demon. Greek philosophy, even at its best in Plato and Aristotle, rejecting a mean and narrow hedonism, nonetheless is founded on a broad and noble one. Praxiteles' Hermes, whose marble torso glows like skin, is carved in such a figure that the eye is forced down to the cold, infecund loins; it is the pederastic lust infecting all Greek art and athletics, spoiling even Plato's finest poetry. But look at John the Baptist, shouldering the lamb, dressed chastely as he stands among the Prophets along the North Portal at Chartres. There the eye

9

is drawn beyond him to the fecund Virgin holding Christ, the Lamb of God Who taketh away the sins of the world. The greatest Greek art — let alone the Hindu — is disordered by a primacy of the sensual. Hector himself, that best of all non-Christian family men, could not answer the arguments of Paris, who said each has his gift, some from Zeus, some from Ares, some from Aphrodite. Beauty when divorced from the good is worse than ugliness because the more seductive. All those

> . . . Godlike shapes and forms
> Excelling human; Princely Dignities,
> And Powers that earst in Heaven sat on Thrones;
> Though of thir Names in heav'nly Records now
> Be no memorial, blotted out and ras'd
> By thir Rebellion, from the Books of Life.
> First Moloch, horrid King besmeard with blood
> Of human sacrifice, and parents tears . . .

Through the hideous litany of Egyptian and Mesopotamian gods, Baalim, Ashtaroth, Thammuz, Dagon, and the rest, Milton proceeds to the slimy prince of Sodom:

> . . . then whom a Spirit more lewd
> Fell not from Heaven, or more gross to love
> Vice for it self: To him no Temple stood
> Or Altar smoak'd; yet who more oft then hee
> In Temples and at Altars, when the Priest
> Turns Atheist, as did Ely's sons, who fill'd
> With lust and violence the house of God.
> In Courts and Palaces he also Reigns
> And in luxurious Cities, where the noise
> Of riot ascends above thir loftiest Tow'rs,
> And injury and outrage: And when Night
> Dark'ns the Streets, then wander forth the Sons
> of Belial, flown with insolence and wine.

But read the daily newspaper:

Liège (UPI) — The prosecution demanded Thursday a

guilty verdict for a young mother, her family and a doctor charged with murdering her armless infant . . . Mrs. Van Put admitted feeding her seven-day-old daughter a lethal dose of honey and barbiturates.

"Sweets to the sweet, farewell!" The following day the headline read: "Doctor's Attorney Brings Court to Tears":

Liège (UPI) — A lawyer defending the doctor accused of prescribing drugs used by a young mother to kill her deformed infant daughter, brought the court to tears Friday. . . . Hundreds of spectators wept openly when attorney Jacques Henry turned to the doctor and said: "You have acted like a man and I am extremely proud that I may call myself your friend." Henry told the jury in his summation that he had known Dr. Casters for thirty years and had grown up with him. He said Dr. Edouard Weerts, the physician who delivered the deformed child, had limited his sympathy for the shocked mother to giving her a sedative and a chair to sit on after she had pleaded with Weerts to kill the infant, named Corinne. "If I had to choose on the moral question, I would rather be in the skin of Dr. Casters than in the skin of Dr. Weerts," Henry said.

"Come, Corinna, come!" — honey on a spoon. And they brought the court to "tears of sympathy."

Defense pleas opened with an appeal to the jury to consult their consciences rather than the articles of the penal code . . . . Arguments developed by the prosecution cannot be appreciated on the basis of the penal code. Your conscience should be your only guide. Speaking in a quiet almost monotonous voice, [the defense attorney] sketched the early life of [Mrs. Van Put] and then described the moment when [she] was first shown her baby. "We all know what a difficult time this woman had giving birth to this child," he said. "We know how terribly she suffered . . . . The few hundred yards she had to walk from her room to the place where her baby was kept have been a real Calvary."

Stabat mater dolorosa. A Calvary indeed, where the Virgin Mary feeds her Son barbiturates and honey? Thoreau said of the then impending crisis that the Mason-Dixon line was across not Virginia but Boston — more accurately, it is drawn across each heart. It is here in each of us, having to do with principles, definitions, penal codes, conscience, and the life and death of little girls. It is no accident that decadence has always led to the hatred of children; no accident that Herod slaughtered the Innocents, that Moloch and the gods of D. H. Lawrence drink human blood in hideous envy of the Eucharist they see with their intelligence but cannot love. It is, of course, no accident that Christ is adored — by shepherds and Magi, the simplest and the most learned — as the Child, who is always present, especially in the thin disguise of an armless infant born in pain. Barbiturates and honey.

Another headline: "Mother, Four Others Are Acquitted."

> Liège (UPI) — An all-male jury Saturday night acquitted a young mother and four other persons of the mercy killing last May of the woman's week-old thalidomide-deformed baby girl. A great roar of approval greeted the verdict in the heavily guarded court when the 12 men voted not guilty after deliberating less than two hours. The court president pounded for order but joyous bedlam reigned.

Jubilation. But not that of the angels and the stars as they sang together on Christmas morning. If there is no room at the inn, is there none in the stable either? Is there no one who could have loved this little girl and understood what a blessing she might have been? The function of the garden of souls is to cultivate not only the great, publicly canonized saints, but the hidden life of sanctity in everyone according to his gifts. This little child had gifts also. It is not that some should live at the expense of others, but that all should be enriched by everyone. This is the economy of the private enterprise of love: it generates. Love is fecund. Love is not only a means to an end, like a road, but is a kind of propulsion. It is like walking up an escalator, or swimming with the current — to beget children, to love children, to encourage their growth, to ease their sufferings, and to suffer oneself with them even to our death. How could they have said, "Kill her, kill her?" And the court concurred, the mob roared its approval, and "joyous bedlam reigned"? No child was ever so deformed as that mother, those doctors, that court, and that crowd. And now the universities and the mass media feed poor girls on honey and barbiturates day and night, injecting all the bitter, anti-Christian doctrine of a lethal liberation, killing warm, admiring, youthful hearts, to leave the husks of lesbians and amazons who hate to cook and sew, whom no young man can love, for whom a child, if it occurs, is called a parasitic growth, scraped into a refuse pail, and rendered into soap.

To beget children, to love her lord in marriage — a woman's work is propelled by joys unsurpassed on earth. They are a figure of the love of the soul for Christ, by which we not only grow but increase and multiply.

The Zero Population Group prefers contraception and abortion because, they say, the world cannot support geometrically increasing numbers of people. They have revived the error of the eighteenth-century amateur sociologist Malthus, who applied the abstract science of geometry to concrete, real, contingent, human — and therefore capricious — beings, which never works. If such and such a trend continues, he said, such and such occurs. But such and such a trend does not continue and surprises undreamt of occur. As it turns out — we know this not by geometric projection but by observation of what has happened — in the first stages of transition from an agricultural to an industrial society, there is a population spurt because medical technology reduces infant deaths. But then fertility falls off as industrialization advances. There are spurts again in times of happiness and hope: a few years' peace after war, prosperity after depression, freedom after totalitarianism. There have even been local jiggles upward when an ice storm breaks the power lines and kills the television set, when husbands and wives discover an unexpected night of happiness and hope away from the latest news.

But the chilling truth is that industrialism brings on a paralyzing gluttony and greed in which the quality of life is quantified. Paradoxically, you cannot afford children in the affluent society. The world has never been so rich and wretched as in these air-conditioned Edens where another child would sap the payments on the second car. There is no population bomb today. Quite the opposite: the question is whether industrialized society can reproduce itself at all.

Malthus said two hundred years ago that population growth would outrun the food supply in England by 1850. He was wildly wrong. By 1850 England had Birmingham and Manchester, with their "dark Satanic mills" — and scientific agriculture. The Zero Population Group predicted mass starvation in India by 1972 — wildly wrong. The Indians have socialism and hybrid grain. Malthusian predictions fail for two reasons: 1) in industrial societies fertility falls; and 2) human beings have intelligence.

They say a finite planet cannot sustain an infinite increase of population. Earth, they say, is like a space ship with limited life supports. But man is part of earth and not merely on it and the planet earth is therefore not a finite globe at all, because when man is multiplied, intelligence is multiplied, infinitely. The life supports are limited only by the intelligence of man; and intelligence is not limited. Josue de Castro, a founder and director of the United Nations Food and Agricultural Organization and one of the five or six world-renowned men in the field of human population problems, put the argument succinctly in a phrase: "Every time a child is born, not just a mouth to feed is born, but hands and brains."

There is no population bomb; and even if there were, even if the wildest geometric projections were true, the world would still be pretty much the same — troubled, risky, polluted, challenging, and good, because as men are multiplied, intelligence and will are multiplied, for better and for worse, richer and poorer. We are always on the razor's edge of glory and annihilation. The population of the world doubled when Eve had two sons; it was cut a fourth by Cain. Today we have looked at Lake Erie and Los Angeles, at hungry people in India, at desperate, unwed pregnant little girls in suburbs, and panicked. What is the cause of ecological and sociological evil? *Men*, we say. *Men* pollute. If you multiply men, since men are wicked, you multiply malice and destruction. Therefore, let us have Zero Population Growth; resist the growth of evil by restricting the birth of men. The traumatic experience of wickedness creates a Hamlet syndrome. When Hamlet found his father murdered by an uncle married to his mother, this rottenness in Denmark, this moral and physical pollution sent him into shock. He said to poor Ophelia: "Get thee to a nunnery. Why wouldst thou be a breeder of sinners?"

Do sane men really think they can lessen wickedness by lessening the number of people? Would greed and lust be satisfied even if only two were left on earth and earth were Paradise? The problem is not the number of people, but what people do. A single Hitler with an atom bomb could waste the world. But in trying to prevent the birth of Hitler, you prevent the birth of Christ. Take the problem up to the highest level, where it belongs. All the rest, what you make of the statistics and the arguments, follows from this: "To be or not to be," as Hamlet also said. And that is not a scientific question. Increase and multiply because each human life reflects uniquely the meaning of the universe. A cripple, a tiny mongoloid that lives if only for a day, an old toothless crone driveling with death but still alive, respond if only with a flicker in the eyes — and that flicker is infinite in value, worth the universe. If we fail to care for that, we need a change of heart. Increase and multiply — of course there is a risk. When brides and grooms make promises till death, they are saying something radically audacious that no geometer can measure, no science comprehend. Love is an act of generosity, the root of which is "generate," because intelligent life is the greatest good in nature. We want more children because the good is diffusive and love increases by giving. Come what will, come what may, whatever the risk, it is a risk of certainty that human life is good. The more the merrier.

> The fig tree puts forth its figs, and the vines, in bloom, give forth fragrance. Arise, my beloved, my beautiful one, and come.

III

In the ordinary daily life of men in Christian culture, who work not only in the sweat of their brows, but for the love of their families, there is also love of work. When men cut wood or go to war or make love to their wives, or when women spin or wash and reciprocate that love, they are working not only to get the job done so that children will be born and grow and have clothes to wear and food to eat. They are working so that those children will one day be saints in heaven. They are working as the very instruments of God's love to create a kind of heavenly garden here and now in the home, by which each axe becomes a violin, each loom a harp, each day a prayer, each hour a psalm.

The skeptic says, "Show me." And we reply, *There*. There, every-where on farms, workshops, homes, even in universities and even — especially — in little cribs where the crippled children lie. This judge, this woman, this doctor, this father — where was the father? Where was that poor, distracted woman's husband, who might have said, "This is my beloved," when the Belgian court, amid a "joyous bed-lam," drank her blood?

John Meynard Keynes proclaimed the economic gospel of the times when he said:

> Avarice and usury and precaution must be our gods for a little longer still. For only they can lead us out of the tunnel of economic necessity into daylight.[1]

According to this view, all men will be happy and good only when all men are rich. To cure war, crime, violence, hatred, and every dis-satisfaction, increase the Gross International Product so massively as to have more than enough of everything for absolutely everyone.

Fifteen hundred years ago, Boethius, prime minister of Rome, awaiting execution in a cell under orders from the barbarian dictator, Theodoric, reflected on the enormously gross product of his empire and concluded that the satisfaction of desire would better be achieved by wanting less. The trouble with Keynes — he said it of Epicureans who held the same position — is that since the human mind conceives universal ideas, desires are infinite and greed can never stuff itself enough. Wars are caused not by poor nations but by rich ones; and the greatest crimes are not the consequence of slums but quite the reverse: slums are caused by the genteel criminality that lurks in country clubs and yachts.

By analogy, the Keynesian educationist thinks the way to happi-ness of mind is through the gross multiplication of knowledge. There will be no ignorance, he says, when all men read all books on every subject, and the whole world becomes an experimental laboratory; whereas Socrates said the highest wisdom is to know that you know nothing, and St. Paul that the wisdom of the world is folly.

Every student wants a good education; parents and taxpayers who

---

[1]See E. F. Schumacher, *Small Is Beautiful*, London, 1973.

pay the tuition want colleges to give them one. But is it the only aim of education to teach youth how to be good scientists and businessmen? Have we forgotten the long tradition of "the best that has been thought and said," in Arnold's phrase, that necessary corrective to the grossly materialistic view that has become, against the explicit command of the Constitution, the established religion of the United States? The long tradition of Western civilization says that education is the acquisition of not only a skill but a discipline, which in turn means not the exercise of the heart, soul, strength, and mind in the service of our appetites, but the subjection of our appetites to the rule of intelligence. Perhaps the purpose of science, business, and knowledge itself is not the conquest of nature after all, but rather that through understanding nature we might come to the conquest of ourselves.

As long as doing what we will does not mean doing His will, we simply will not see the fact of God's existence and presence. God is not an idea, or a theory to be demonstrated, or a symbol to be translated into the latest style, or even an ideal of perfection: He is a person, really existing here and now, *ubique semper idem* — everywhere always the same. And as He exists, He works. You can know *that* God is by philosophy, and *Who* He is by faith; but to know Him *as* He is, to "walk and talk" with Him as the old hymn says, is to practice what the spiritual writers call "custody of the heart," to glance within ourselves and see. "Be still and know that I am God." This is not to study or to teach just another subject in the curriculum, but to place God where He is, at the beginning and end of every work, and to live in Him, reminded of Him all day long, so that a woman may touch her wedding ring in the middle of her household cares and say, "My Lord, my husband — and our God." Opposed to this sits the cannibal Mr. Kurtz, licking his bloody lips in the jungle, who will never marry his "intended." In the absence of culture you do not get lovely wild grass. If you cease to cultivate, you rot. Belgium is rotting. The whole Christian West is rotting. The romantic dream that "consenting adults" left to themselves will come to good is rotten nonsense, contradicted by the continuous experience of history and everyday life. Nor can we solve the problem of the poor by misconstruing the dictum that men cannot live by bread alone to mean that they must have cake. Liberal Christianity is death by socialism. Without the Bread of Life — barbiturates and honey.

The restoration of Christian culture is the restoration of *all things* in Christ and especially the restoration of the spirit of Christ: poverty of heart, fecundity in our loins.

To put the choice in another example, let us consider a pitifully misguided — one hopes forgivable — young man who confused the love of God with a vicious sentimentality, and in the name of one of the greatest saints.

The first from an essay in a popular religious magazine by an ex-seminarian who left the Jesuit order because, he says, "Every Jesuit, according to the eleventh rule of the summary of the constitutions, is required to share in the contempt and the cross of Christ." This means, he says, that every Jesuit must therefore literally "be a scandal to his own brethren and even cast out of the Society as a madcap. To be Christlike means to be disowned by our own community, to be, as it were, disinherited by heaven." Of course we are back — what a bore it is — once more at a contradiction: to be a Jesuit one must be a non-Jesuit; to be a Christian, one must be a non-Christian. In the peroration of the essay, the ex-seminarian says that God's "is a holiness that transcends the distinction 'saint-sinner.' " And there we have that total contradiction in parody, which always must result in jubilations like that of the Belgian court — the smiling face of what seems like a forgivable sentimentality stripped to its true horror and death. The transcending of real distinctions in disobedience to the law of contradiction is one of the major marks of Modernism. It is not only a denial of philosophical truth; it is a denial of the Truth Himself. It is satanic, obliterating good and evil. If you transcend the distinction between saint and sinner, you commit sin. Our ex-seminarian and ex-Christian concludes:

> No man will want to go to heaven if heaven is a place where we have to stand on needle-points before the Universal Emperor. Which soldier would like to be always in the presence of his commanding officer?

The answer is, of course, the good soldier, and certainly the Jesuit soldier of Christ — custody of heart, as St. Ignatius explains, is precisely standing "always in the presence" of the Universal Emperor.

18

Which seminarian would like to spend all his years under the nose of his bishop?

The answer is the seminarian who, like St. John, leaned on the breast of his beloved Lord.

> If people revolt against the idea of God as a monarch in whose presence the subjects cannot be at ease, it is nothing surprising. If they are not enthusiastic about a heaven where they have to stand at attention or march with "eyes right" it is quite understandable. The plain truth is, that is not God; that is not heaven. God is He in whom our hearts find rest . . . It is in love that one can be at ease . . . . I have seen pictures of saints with their eyes cast down, or fixed in a stare. If heaven is a place where we have to keep on staring at God, it is certainly a loathsome place.

Sanity, Frank Sheed says, is the health of the intellect. It is seeing what is really before us, as sanctity is the health of the will, loving what we really see; and theology, he says, is the science of sanity. We can see in the confusion of this wretched young man the attempt to love God without intelligence, with emotions only. *Ars sine scientia nihil.* Art, including the art of sanctity, is nothing without knowledge. The attempt to reach a mystical identification of self and God without theology is at best quietism and at worst the total wreck of religion as it is found in Hinduism and Buddhism, with their doctrines of universal sympathy and the transcending of real distinctions. Love is based on a distinction. Love is a relation not of identity but of will. Man is a creature; he is not God, just as a husband is a man and his wife a woman and neither can "play the role" of the other. A father is an adult and not a child, and all men, women, and children are creatures put on earth, as Blake says, "to learn to bear the beams of love," whose dimmest success is a brilliant clarity in which distinctions are made, not broken.

2 The Perennial Heresy[2]

The Modernist movement in literature, now about one hundred years old, is no longer merely the contemporary or current. It is rather a definable period in cultural history. Though terms like Neoclassic or Romantic are difficult to define, still, unless we admit that history is the nightmare Joyce's Stephen Daedalus thought it was, we must work with categories. Romantic and Neoclassic are necessary, though difficult, terms and the same is true of Modern, which describes that period in our cultural history beginning in 1857 and ending . . . very shortly, one suspects. The particular choice of year is somewhat arbitrary, of course — Marx published in 1848 and Darwin in 1859 — but from the literary point of view the birth of *Les fleurs du mal* and *Madame Bovary* takes precedence.

The consequences of these events reached their majority by the turn of the century, their maturity by World War I, the full expansion of middle-aged ripeness in the 1920s; and we are now into advanced old age where evidences of senility appear in the latest cinematic shocks and the *graffiti* novel — garrulous recollections of Modernism's childhood in the work of Baudelaire or Isidore Ducasse, the bogus Comte de Laturéamont.

The present essay makes no attempt to prove that Modernism exists, but proceeding at once on the obvious fact that it does, analyzes two of its essential characteristics, interlocked and reciprocally causative, not mere aspects of Modernism, but the very valves of its heart — *artificiality* and *sensationalism*. Clarifications if not definitions of

---

[2]A significant part of this chapter appeared in *University of Wyoming Publications*, 25:3 (1961).

these terms will proceed along with their application.

With due respect to its failures — for it seems to be failing now — the triumph of three thousand years of Western civilization has been, from the point of view of ideas, the philosophy vaguely called Realism or the Perennial Philosophy, because it has survived so many seasons. It may be summed up in a sentence: *The real is really real;* or in a word — *is*. The terse scholastic formula defines it: *Demonstrationis principium 'quod quid est'* — the beginning of proof is 'that which is'; or in another: *Veritas sequitur esse rerum* — truth follows upon the existence of things. According to this view, the principle of all things is "to be." *In principio erat Verbum.* In the beginning was — not the Word — but the Verb, to which all verbs and nouns as well are ultimately reducible. "I am that I am," said God.

The capital text in philosophy is Aristotle's, which sums up Socrates, Plato, and all antecedent and subsequent Realists — quite simply the most important chapter in the history of metaphysics:

> It is impossible for the same attribute at once to belong and not to belong to the same thing and in the same relation . . . . This is the most certain of all principles . . . for it is impossible for anyone to suppose that a thing is and is not . . . .
>
> Hence all men who are demonstrating anything refer back to this as an ultimate belief; for it is by nature the starting point of all the other axioms as well.
>
> There are some, however . . . who both state themselves that the same thing can be, and not be, and say that it is possible to hold this view. Many even of the physicists adopt this theory . . . . We can demonstrate the impossibility by refutation, if only our opponent makes some statement. If he makes none, it is absurd to seek for an argument against one who has no arguments of his own about anything . . . for such a person, in so far as he is such, is really no better than a vegetable . . . . The starting point for all such discussions is not the claim that he should state that something is or is not so (because that might be supposed to be a begging of the question), but that he should say something significant both to himself and to another (this is essential if any argument is to

21

follow; for otherwise such a person cannot reason either with himself or with another) . . . . Thus in the first place it is obvious that this at any rate is true: that the term "to be" or "not to be" has definite meaning; so that not everything can be "so and not so" . . . . For if it is equally possible to assert or deny anything of anything, one thing will not differ from another; for if anything differs, it will be true and unique . . . . Moreover it follows that all statements would be true and all false; and that our opponent himself admits that what he says is false. Besides it is obvious that discussion with him is pointless, because he makes no real statement.[3]

All of this is simply common sense raised to philosophical perfection. It is the normal mind's first reaction to the world — to know that it exists. Before he reflects, that is, "bends back" his attention to his own mental and sensory processes, a man first simply looks, smells, tastes, touches, and affirms existence. Not *Cogito ergo sum;* but *Aliquid est, intelligo, ergo sum et ergo cogito.* Something exists and I know it and therefore I know that I exist and think. Thinking follows from existence; it does not make things so.

As Aristotle says, anyone denying this, denies his own denial. Make any statement at all and you have affirmed the existence of what it is you have said, either possibly or really. The man who says, "This lie is true," has neither lied nor told the truth. He has said nothing at all. The famous "contradiction card" on one face says, "The statement on the other side of this card is true"; and when you turn it over it says, "The statement on the other side of this card is false."

George Orwell, a Modernist himself at the late stage, criticized much more than socialism in *1984:*

It was as though some huge force were pressing down upon you — something that penetrated inside your skull, battering against your brain, frightening you out of your beliefs, persuading you almost to deny the evidence of your senses. In the end the Party would announce that

---

[3]*Metaphysics* IV. Translation by A. T. Murray, Loeb Library.

two and two made five, and you would have to believe it.
It was inevitable that they should make that claim sooner
or later: the logic of their position demanded it. Not
merely the validity of experience but the very existence of
external reality was tacitly denied by their philosophy.
The heresy of heresies was common sense . . . . The
Party told you to reject the evidence of your eyes and ears.
It was their final, most essential command . . . . And yet
he was right! They were wrong and he was right. The
obvious, the silly, the true, had got to be defended.
Truisms are true, hold on to that! . . . Stones are hard,
water is wet, objects unsupported fall toward the earth's
center. With the feeling . . . that he was setting forth an
important axiom, he wrote: Freedom is the freedom to say
that two plus two make four. If that is granted, all else
follows.

The poor lost functionary in the fabricated world of 1984 rediscovers
the Perennial Philosophy. Orwell is one of the first popular writers,
emerging from the heart of Marxism, to see this essential fact about
Modernism — that it is an assault upon the verb "to be," that its
formal cause is "artificiality," the first of the two interlocking principles asserted of it in this essay.

Aristotle, master of himself in most cases, almost loses his temper
over this. He calls the sophists "vegetables," and finally liars:

It is quite evident that no one, either of those who profess
this theory or of any other school, is *really* in this position.
Otherwise, why does a man walk to Megara and not stay
at home, when he thinks he ought to make the journey?
Why does he not walk early one morning into a well or a
ravine, if he comes to it, instead of clearly guarding against
doing so, thus showing that he does *not* think that it is
equally good and not good to fall in?

But ding dong bell, pussy's in the well! Though you cannot refute
Aristotle, you can deliberately choose to drown. J. K. Huysmans, the
paradigm of literary anti-Realism, in his novel *A Rebours* — "Against"
— describes the dining room of his hero Des Esseintes, the perfect
Modernist, which

23

resembled a ship's cabin, with its ceiling of arched beams, its bulkheads and floor-boards of pitch-pine, and the little window-opening, let into the wainscotting like a porthole . . . [behind which] was a large aquarium . . . . Thus what daylight penetrated into the cabin had at first to pass through . . . the waters . . . . He could then imagine himself between decks in a brig, and gaze inquisitively at some ingenious mechanical fishes driven by clockwork, which moved backwards and forwards behind the port-hole window and got entangled in artificial seaweed. At other times, while he was inhaling the smell of tar which had been introduced into the room before he entered it, he would examine a series of colour prints on the walls, such as you see in packet-boat offices and Lloyd's agencies, representing steamers bound for Valparaiso and the River Plate . . . . By these means he was able to enjoy quickly, almost simultaneously, all the sensations of a long sea-voyage, without ever leaving home . . . . The imagination could provide a more than adequate substitute for the vulgar reality of actual experience.

Aristotle flings his challenge to the physicists: If you deny the law of contradiction, why walk to Megara when you want to go there? Huysmans replies: "I don't." And he proceeds one step further in describing the particular techniques for the surpassing of reality in imagination:

The main thing is to know how to set about it, to be able to concentrate your attention on a single detail, to forget yourself sufficiently to bring about the desired hallucina-tion and substitute the vision of a reality for the reality itself . . . . There can be no shadow of doubt that with her never-ending platitudes the old Crone [Nature] has by now exhausted the good-humored admiration of all true artists, and the time has surely come for artifice to take her place wherever possible.

Aristotle said art is the imitation of nature; Huysmans' art surpasses her.

24

After all, to take what among her works is considered to be the most exquisite, what among all her creations is deemed to possess the most perfect and original beauty — to wit, woman — has not man, for his part, by his own efforts, produced an animate, yet artificial creature that is every bit as good from the point of view of plastic beauty? Does there exist anywhere on this earth a being born in the throes of motherhood, who is more dazzlingly, more outstandingly beautiful than the two locomotives recently put into service on the Northern Railway?

The whole of modernist aesthetic is in this obviously ridiculous but most serious — not at all satiric — passage. Huysmans has suggested that we concentrate by a kind of artistic yoga on a single detail — what is usually called the symbol — in order to annihilate reality. And then he goes one crucial stage further: after the achievement of unconsciousness, he reconstructs his own false consciousness, a deliberate, self-induced hallucination.

To the Party, Orwell said, "Orthodoxy is unconsciousness." Huysmans goes on beyond unconsciousness. He saw that the opposite of Being is not just nothing — the mere absence of Being, like empty space, which has a kind of ablative reality, a potential for being filled. Pure non-Being, antibeing, is the *faking of reality*.

Ortega y Gasset formulated the modern crisis in precisely these terms in *The Dehumanization of Art:*

The progressive dis-realization of the world, which began in the philosophy of the Renaissance, reaches its extreme consequence in the radical sensationalism of Avenarius and Mach. How can this continue? What new philosophy is possible? A return to primitive realism is unthinkable; four centuries of criticism, of doubt, of suspicion, have made this attitude forever untenable. To remain in our subjectivism is equally impossible. Where shall we find the material to reconstruct the world?

Note that in rejecting criticism and doubt, he nonetheless accepts the consequences. That is, he does not attempt to refute an error but, conceding a change in fashion, rather like Monsieur Ennui in

25

Baudelaire, "stifles" the philosophy of Realism in a four-hundred-year-old yawn. Nowhere does he or anyone else in this position ever find an answer to Aristotle within the terms of reason. It is not that they have committed an error; they have abandoned the intelligence.

> The philosopher retracts his attention even more and, instead of directing it to the subjective as such, fixes on what up to now has been called "the content of consciousness," that is, the intra-subjective. There may be no corresponding reality to what our ideas project and what our thoughts think, but this does not make them purely subjective. A world of hallucination would not be real, but neither would it fail to be a world, an objective universe, full of sense and perfection. Although the imaginary centaur does not really gallop, tail and mane in the wind, across real prairies, he has a peculiar independence with regard to the subject that imagines him. He is a virtual object, or, as the most recent philosophy expresses it, an ideal object. This is the type of phenomena which the thinker of our time considers most adequate as a basis for his universal system. Can we fail to be surprised at the coincidence between such a philosophy and its synchronous art, known as expressionism or cubism?

Ortega for fifty years was what a good cultural journalist should be, a weathervane for doctrines; and in this particular passage he has pointed out the direction of the prevailing winds. He has seen that culture is integral. As an organic growth, all its parts — music, painting, literature, science, politics, philosophy, religion — move and work as one. The purpose of this present essay is to get behind appearances to the source. Knowledge, Aristotle says, is necessarily of causes. Ortega's very brilliance is the shining of a flaw because like all Modernists he is convinced there are no causes, only winds.

In the work of Baudelaire, the first and greatest master of the Modernist movement, the poem is neither the expression of ideas, as the Classicist would have it, nor the expression of the emotions, as the Romanticist would have it — the poem is the expression of nothing but the poem itself. This famous *art pour l'art*, announced but never tried by Gautier, was put into practice, though without success, by

Baudelaire and the Parnassians. The slightest examination of the contents of such "pure poetry" shows that the poem is not really a thing in itself, as it claims, but rather a vehicle for the doctrine that poems ought to be taken as things in themselves. Modernists preach what they do not practice. Baudelaire's enameled verse states but never achieves its purpose because his poems do have meaning; the meaning is that there is no meaning to either poems or anything else.

The Neoclassicist thought of poems as artificial constructions — as conventional systems of words and phrases. But he thought the function of this artificial convention was to carry true ideas: what was "often thought but ne'er so well expressed." The Romantic thought of himself as an Aeolian harp, a sensitive instrument tuned to the unseen presences in himself. The poem was to express "intense emotion recollected in tranquility." The function of the Modernist poem is to rid ourselves first of thought and next of emotion, so that we achieve that orthodoxy Orwell spoke of as "unconsciousness." And then, at the second stage, the poet, as magician, creates upon this absence of idea and emotion the pure artifice of the work of art as a thing in itself.

Compare the typical Romantic poem of the sea voyage with Baudelaire's major work, "Le voyage." Alfred de Vigny, in "La bouteille à la mer," tells of a shipwrecked captain who in a final gesture of triumph over malevolent fate flings on the waves a sealed bottle containing the precious manuscript of his intense if not tranquil recollections, which somehow, sometime will find their way to port.

> *Puis, receuillant le fruit tel que de l'âme il sort,*
> *Tout empreint du parfum des saintes solitudes,*
> *Jetons l'oeuvre à la mer, la mer des multitudes:*
> *— Dieu la prendra du doigt pour la conduire au port.*

> Then plucking the fruit as it grows from the soul,
> Marked with the perfume of holy solitudes,
> Let us throw the work to the sea, the sea of the multitudes:
> — God will touch it with his finger, bringing it to port.

Vigny's young, Romantic captain smiles at death.

Baudelaire's old Captain is Death himself. Victory, for Baudelaire, is the annihilation of success, because — and this is the really striking difference between the Romantic and the Modernist — Baudelaire's voyage never takes place. As Huysmans said, the best voyages are imaginary. At the very start of the Modernist arc we find this restlessness without purpose, as near the end it survives in the jargon of the beatnik motorcyclists: "Let's go, man, go" — nowhere in particular, but just go. *Part pour partir* is the theme of all true voyagers, Baudelaire says; or, as he said in another poem, quoting Poe, it is to go "anywhere out of this world." For Baudelaire the ship is not real. It is an imaginary projection of himself, as it is in Rimbaud's "Le bateau ivre," or Mallarmé's "Un coup de dès," or Dylan Thomas' "Ballad of the Long-Legged Bait." Baudelaire expressly says so:

> *Notre âme est un trois-mâts cherchant son Icarie . . .*
> *Chaque îlot signalé par l'homme de vigie*
> *Est un Eldorado promis par le Destin;*
> *L'Imagination qui dresse son orgie*
> *Ne trouve qu'un récif aux clartés du matin.*
> *Ô le pauvre amoureux des pays chimériques! . . .*
> *Ce matelot ivrogne, inventeur d'Amériques.*

> Our soul is a three-masted schooner searching its
>   Icaria . . .
> Each islet, signaled by the lookout,
> Is an Eldorado promised by destiny;
> The imagination that prepares its orgy
> Finds only a reef in the light of dawn.
> O poor lover of chimerical nations —
> This drunken sailor, inventor of Americas.

But why should he invent Americas? If everything is in one's head, why go on voyages at all, even imaginary ones? Des Esseintes never asked. But Baudelaire replies:

> *Au fond de l'inconnu pour trouver du nouveau!*
> In the depths of the unknown to find the new!

Le nouveau! The motive force of Modernism is, as the name suggests, the perpetual urge for the new — not the real, not the true, not the ideal, not even the evil, not the power or the glory or the lust, but all these things for the sake of the new. Cut off from reality by "four hundred years of criticism and doubt," the Modernist, insisting on the new, very quickly exhausts the contents of his memory and proceeds to invent an artificial one. The image — that is, what the "imagination" produces — substitutes for Being. To the Realist, an image must necessarily be *of* something; and the something can be understood in terms of ideas and feelings. The Modernist, cut off from reality, has nothing but the image, nothing but the mental sensation. Huysmans never said he could imagine a real voyage; he said he could have all the sensations of a real voyage. The Realist asks, "What is the image of?" For art holds the mirror up to nature. The Modernist, a worshipper of Baal in more than one way, replies, "There is nothing but the image." He is a worshipper of images.

The "dis-realization" of the universe — the pursuit of artificiality — leads to the second of the marks of Modernism, sensationalism. The physicists, whom Aristotle lost his temper at, concentrated on truth as that which is sensed. They were drawn inevitably to the next step, the experiment. But experiment becomes an artifice. Empiricism began with an explicit rejection of Realism in the Renaissance — an explicit attack on Aristotle — and with the wholly unexamined assumption that the real is the quantitative; that is, the real is what can be measured. At first sight, it would seem as if science were affirming Aristotle, affirming the evidence of the senses. Quite the contrary, however: it affirmed the evidence of appearances divorced from substance. By considering the truth to be only what is sensed, science lays itself open to the psychologizing of knowledge. If truth is only what is sensed, and sensations happen in the mind, then truth is in the mind — and not, as Aristotle said, a real relation of the mind and thing. Orwell added: "And if the mind can be controlled — what then?"

The consequence of Empiricism is phenomenology, in which the experiment itself becomes a hallucination. Though in the early stages of science an experiment was set up to test a reality supposed to exist outside the test, in the latest stage the test is often taken not as the result *of* anything, but the only reality there is, so that one cannot challenge the validity of an intelligence test, for example, because intelligence is by definition whatever it is the test tests. Science at this stage has become magic, a false sacrament effecting what it signifies. It is no longer the "adequation of the mind to reality" but a mental construction for "saving the appearances" and finally an instrument of aesthetic pleasure. Science for science's sake.

Ernst Mach, for example, the founder of Empirio-Criticism and one of the great physicists of his day — the Mach unit of sound velocity is named for him — in his *Contribution to the Analysis of Sensations* denies the existence of the person experiencing the experiment.

> The primary fact is not the *I*, the ego, but the sensations. The elements that constitute the *I*. "I have the sensation green," signifies that the element green occurs in a given complex of other elements (sensations, memories). When I cease to have the sensation green, when I die, then the elements no longer occur in their ordinary, familiar way of association. That is all. Only an ideal mental-economical unit, not a real unity, has ceased to exist.

The divorce from Realism gives us two possibilities to exploit. First, the piling up of empirical evidence without regard to intelligence at all. Seeing is believing — that is to say, reality is appearance. Jean-Paul Sartre prints this phrase without a quiver in his essay significantly titled *Being and Nothingness:* "Appearance is essence." The word "existence" among such existentialists is used as the Party uses words like "love" and "peace" — to mean its direct opposite. The second possibility after the great divorce is Rationalism. Descartes, its progenitor, argues that we know nothing but what is in our minds, all sense experience being merely an extension of mentality. His metaphysics begins, opposite to Aristotle's, not with Being, but with the *cogito* — with thought. Sense objects are reified ideas.

According to Whitehead, modern philosophy is the development of these two horns, both stemming from the one head of anti-Realism. Whereas Aristotelian tradition maintained that truth is the real relation between mind and thing, modern philosophy has maintained from two different points of view that truth is either mind or thing. What Whitehead calls the "great bifurcation" split the world into two quarreling *but allied* armies fighting on the same side against Realism — the Empiricist and the Rationalist. Kant lumped them together under "the Critical." In the Modernistic age the armies have at last been reunited as "Empirio-Criticism" or "Phenomenalism."

In a prophetic paragraph of that same Book IV of the *Metaphysics*, Aristotle fixes the necessary connection between sensationalism and nonbeing. Speaking again of those who argue that things can both be and not be, he says:

> They say that the same thing seems sweet to some who taste it, and bitter to others; so that if all men were diseased or all insane, except two or three who were healthy or sane, the latter would seem to be diseased or insane, and not the others. [Orwell's Winston Smith had wondered about his sanity.] And further they say that many of the animals as well get from the same things impressions which are true or false; for one kind is no more true than another, but equally so. And hence Democritus says that either there is no truth or we cannot discover it. And in general, it is because they suppose that thought is sense-perception . . . . The reason why these men hold this view is that . . . they supposed that reality is confined to sensible things.
>
> All these theories destroy the possibility of anything's existing by necessity because they destroy the existence of its essence; for the necessary cannot be in one way and in another; and so if anything exists of necessity, it cannot be both so and not so.

Art for art's sake, science for science's sake — the worshipping of graven images, and therefore the worshipping of unreality. An image is the mental reproduction of something sensed; its reality derives from two necessarily existing things: the subject who does the sensing, and the object that is sensed. The purely mental world of the image sensation has no more being than an image in a mirror. The idea of what Ortega called the *intrasubjective*, or the "ideal object," is a fiction. If you cut off reality from the image and take the image in itself, you have not changed the nature of imagery but, transferring it from the garden to the parlor, have killed it and put it in a jar to new use. An image is still a mental sensation; you have become interested in the mental act rather than the purpose of the mental act. We become aware of sensation *qua* sensation only by reflection. Normally we go directly to the thing: we say ice is cold, not that we have a sensation of coldness, or, to use Orwell's examples, we say that "stones are hard, water is wet." Once the divorce is made, however, we can suspend the mind, hold it back forcibly from its completion in the object, and consider the sensation in itself. Art for art's sake is a sterilization of the mind so as to prevent "conception" while enjoying discourse.

But the nature of imagery is not changed by the use to which it is put. Utility is not function. A kind of Larmarckian naiveté pervades some schools of criticism as well as of morality: If you use a thing long enough in a way contrary to its nature, they say, you will eventually change its nature, as if by sitting on tables you could make them chairs. This is a form of thinking makes it so. Phenomenalism is a resuscitated Nominalism that asserts that an image is a reality — that the imagination can construct a real life of its own. Of course it simply cannot. Any sensation divorced from its object withers. Huysmans learned this to his bitter despair, and so did Baudelaire and Rimbaud. Ortega evidently did not, nor have most Moderns, because they talk about it rather than doing it and so they still seek hallucination as a panacea. Those who have tried it know better. In real life ideas have permanence; emotions, durability. But sensations are instantaneous and must be renewed, and in the renewal itself is destruction, because repetition dulls. Thus the sensationalist is doomed to chase *le nouveau*, which must always elude him.

"Et puis? Et puis encore?" "What next? And then what next?" cries Baudelaire's old Captain. Ennui is the hell of Modernism. The aesthetic in the extreme is anaesthetic: numb, having no sensation, unconscious.

"What shall we do? What shall we ever do?" the ladies in *The Waste Land* ask.

In what is perhaps the most famous of all Modernistic poems, Mallarmé's "L'après-midi d'un faun," the Faun compares art to blowing up empty grape skins, which he holds to the light:

> *Ainsi, quand des raisins j'ai sucé la clarté,*
> *Pour bannir un regret par ma feinte écarté,*
> *Rieur, j'élève au ciel d'eté la grappe vide*
> *Et, soufflant dans ses peaux lumineuses, avide*
> *D'ivresse, jusqu'au soir je regarde au travers.*

> Thus when I have sucked the brightness from grapes,
> To banish a regret set aside by my pretense,

Laughing, I raise to the summer sky the empty cluster,
And blowing into their luminous skins, avid
For drunkenness, I watch through the skins until
    evening.

Having sucked out the pulp of reality, he is left with the pure, detached image, not *of* anything. A logical extension of this idea is the enjoyment of the poem as typography, as the pure sensation of the skin of the printed page, in Mallarmé's last and most ambitious work, "Coup de dès," and the imitations by e. e. cummings and others.

Less extreme, but with the same intention, is Imagism, the school of poetry devoted to surfaces in which neither thought nor emotion is supposed to intrude. When Archibald MacLeish says

    A poem should be palpable and mute
    As a globed fruit . . .
        A poem should not mean
    But be

he is reducing the poem to sensation, his globed fruit very like the Faun's empty grape skin. He has deprived the verb "to be" of its real pulp. He does not really mean "be"; he means "sensed."

Imagism is sensationalism. Baudelaire, its first and greatest practitioner, is more interested in his mistress' skin than in his mistress, and, even further, in her hair, her fingernails, finally in the polish on her fingernails, her jewels, her perfume. The scandal at the publication of *Les fleurs du mal* was misplaced because Baudelaire is not simply a great pornographic poet like Keats, for example. Baudelaire's poems do not use the senses to excite concupiscence. Quite the contrary, they detach the sensation from both cause and consequence, from both the pulp of the grape and the wine. Baudelaire is, as the Modernist jazz musicians say, "cool." "All mastery is cold," said Mallarmé; and he speaks in his letters of having climbed "pure glaciers of aesthetic."

The most thorough experiment in sensationalism is Proust's. *A la recherche du temps perdu* is seven volumes of recaptured — not "remembered," but "researched" — sensations. Not intense emotion recollected in tranquility, but intense emotion tranquilized in recollection. The *déjà vu* experience of the notorious macaroon at the start of

33

Swann's Way is the key to Proust's whole work. The philosophy behind it is Phenomenalism. Since reality is nothing but sensation, art can create reality by means of invoking sensations. Needless to say, the pitiful, debauched lives of his characters — they are caricatures, cartoons — prove their own vacuity; they are exhausted bladders, emptied skins, at the end, having collapsed into the Baudelairian ennui. The pathos of the dying Swann, left alone by his Duchess in search of a shoe, is the revelation that sensation cut off from reality is illusion. Swann is aptly named after the most widely used symbolist bird, whose meaning is "the artist," the fabricator of illusions. Swann's "way" is the *via ludens*, the way of the artificer, which is to say the magician who hallucinates sensations.

The absolute extreme of artificiality and sensationalism is *maya*, the Oriental doctrine of the world itself as illusion. If reality is sensation, it follows that since sensations can be invoked in the absence of objects, as in hallucination, we can as well act as if objects themselves are hallucinations evoked by other magicians or demons. This is not Platonism. The magician does not believe in the permanent reality of his constructions. He does not believe in the independent, permanent, immutable existence of intellectual forms as the exemplars of his constructions. His universe is not only immaterial, it is insubstantial. He never leaves Plato's Cave. Between the world of Platonic forms and the world of sense objects lies magic, the creation of the Hermetic artist. Magic is the manipulation of sensations detached from their objects. The original bifurcation of Rationalism and Empiricism has reached its end at last in the realm of fantasy.

It is not necessary to document the extraordinary interest modern culture has had in Oriental ideas. As a matter of fact, we can read our own future in the East. Yoga is the exact science of what is as yet only a parlor game with us. It is the science of hallucination. It is practiced by the techniques Huysmans only fooled with, by what Rimbaud, in one of the most influential documents in modern literature, called "the deliberate derangement of the senses." Whether by shallow breathing, which cuts off oxygen to the brain, thus causing it to malfunction; or by constrictive postures, which affect the blood and lymph systems; by fasting, drugs, and, above all, self-hypnosis induced by *mantra* — the repetition of sounds — or *yantra* — the gazing on intricate geometrical patterns — or by *koan* — the Japanese system of thinking about logical impossibilities — by any and all these devices the yogi is able to break through his own normal experience of the world.

The meaning of the Hindu word *moksha* is "breakthrough," "release." This breakthrough is at first an experience of the Baudelarian hell of ennui, or nonsensation, of the Party's "unconscious orthodoxy." But following this is the second stage of the re-release, the Great Liberation, the "awakening" after the unconsciousness. The word *Buddha* means "awake." This is the state of hallucination in which the Buddha has the power to construct any "reality" he wants. The power is supposed to be such that the hallucination can be imposed on others. Walls can be "imagined" that not only the magician, but his audience cannot walk through. Palaces are said to be constructed in which we may wine and dine. And, conversely, according to this doctrine, since the real world is only an hallucination imposed by the demon-magician, whom Christians call the Word, then by our own counteracting will we can walk through real walls, and real palaces can be destroyed, real mountains can be moved, fire eaten, water walked upon.

In point of fact, the mountains of the *mind* are moved, its palaces destroyed. Buddhahood is the supreme insanity. It is not just the wreckage of certain mental functions that we find in psychiatric wards, but the perfect destruction of the whole mind altogether. The Buddha does not dwell under the delusion that he is Napoleon, or even that he is Buddha. He dwells under the supreme delusion that everything is a delusion — that Napoleon was a paranoiac under the delusion that he was Napoleon, God a paranoiac demon under the delusion that He is God. There is no Buddhist God, but pantheons of idols; daimons and demons, all shapes and misshapes, maidens and monstrosities with eight arms and four heads, smiling, leering, erotically suggestive, bleeding, devouring, rotting. Beyond the hell of ennui — we should say limbo, for it is a shallow place compared with this — is the deep hell of hallucination.

The final point is at once the most difficult and shocking, and it sums up all the rest: According to the Perennial Philosophy, the universe begins with Being. And further, according to this tradition also, Being is good. *Ens et bonum convertuntur.* Being and good are convertible terms. Evil is therefore non-Being. Evil is the privation of good. It follows therefore that insofar as one is cut off from Being, he is cut off from good. There is what we may call a law of gravity of artificiality. The universe of hallucination cannot be pleasant for long. It is inevitably hell that the artificer constructs. That is why in the pantheon of idols the hideous predominates.

The skin of Baudelaire's *venus noire* is not very far from the skin stretched on the Witch of Buchenwald's lampshade. The divorce from *reality* is a divorce also from *morality*, because good and bad are matters of intellectual judgment about things. As Aristotle explained in the passages cited, the reduction of reality to sensation does away with difference in essence. And if everything happens accidentally, there is no right and wrong. From the point of view of the history of men, rather than of ideas, "disrealization" (as Ortega saw) becomes dehumanization. Recall Ernst Mach demonstrating that since reality is sensation, there is no such thing as a human being. The experimenter disappears in the experiment. The man dissolves into an accidental bundle of sensations, exactly as Baudelaire's mistress dissolves into her jewels, or Picasso's models into lines and blocks. Rimbaud acted out the poems of Baudelaire in everyday life to the point of committing crimes. He was not the *hypocrite lecteur* at least. In a prophetic line he cried, "Now is the time of the assassins."

Behind the shifting mask of Modernism — behind the reciprocal principles of artificiality and sensationalism — is the diabolic. The perfection of nonbeing is the lie. Just plain nothing has a reality. Absence in itself is not evil. It is the deliberate activity of absence that is evil. Not merely doing nothing, but, to make the meaning clear by emphasis, it is *doing* nothing. A lie is not the mere absence of the truth, not silence, but the active assertion of what is not the truth. Satan, Prince of Lies, is called the Ape of God. The perfection of nonbeing is parody.

Truth follows upon the existence of things. And not only truth, but falsehood as well. This is not a quarrel of words. This is not hairsplitting. The universe is split, and what is more important — and worth all the universe besides — each man is split, for truth is "sharper than any two-edged sword, even to dividing body and soul asunder."

3 Eastward Ho! — Hum

England at the height of power, Queen of Christendom and all seas, mistress of most land, and Tennyson at his height, master of words, the second Virgil, himself

> Wielder of the stateliest measure
> Ever moulded by the lips of man

— all this was so; and looking back one cannot help being amazed and frightened that England in the memory of our fathers was if not the apex of civilization, at least the solidest, most sensible ruling power since the Antonines, with a chance at last of inaugurating what Christians had always dreamed of, the Christian World State. All this was so, and yet, as some vague Germanic beast haunted the imagination of its greatest poet, something like it, sinister and unnamed, haunted the imagination of the age:

> Below the thunders of the upper deep,
> Far, far beneath in the abysmal sea,
> His ancient, dreamless, uninvaded sleep
> The Kraken sleepeth; faintest sunlights flee
> About his shadowy sides: above him swell
> Huge sponges of millennial growth and height;
> And far away into the sickly light,
> From many a wondrous grot and secret cell
> Unnumber'd and enormous polypi
> Winnow with giant arms the slumbering green.

Arnold called it "the eternal note of sadness"; "exhaustion" would have been more accurate. It is everywhere in Tennyson, visible in his magnificent optical effects which, like Turner's, celebrate a grand but dying light, where the horses of the sun

> Shake the darkness from their loosen'd manes,
> And beat the twilight into flakes of fire.

Actually the beast had first emerged in France to pasture on a decadence further advanced than England's until, strong enough, at the end of the century, he prowled about the world at will. Ennui became exoticism and the paralyzed West began its journey to the East like the dying Alexander on his litter.

> *Amer savoir, celui qu'on tire du voyage!*
> *Le monde, monotone et petit, aujourd'hui,*
> *Hier, demain, toujours, nous fait voir notre image:*
> *Une oasis d'horreur dans un desert d'ennui!*

> Bitter knowledge one gets from travel,
> The world, monotonous and small, today,
> Yesterday, tomorrow, always, shows us our own image:
> An oasis of horror in a desert of ennui.

So much for the world and us, according to Baudelaire. Given this condition, what shall we do?

> *Faut-il partir? Rester? Si tu peux rester, reste;*
> *Pars, s'il le faut. L'un court, et l'autre se tapit*
> *Pour tromper l'ennemi vigilant et funeste;*
> *Le temps!*

> Must we go? Stay? If you can, stay;
> Go if you must. One runs, another crouches
> To fool the vigilant and deadly enemy
> Time!

Note that time is not the subtle thief who steals our youth. On the contrary, he is deadly duration, sad waste of time, time to kill, immortality in which one yearns to die, like Tennyson's Tithonous or the Sibyl in Petronius.

The woods decay, the woods decay and fall,
The vapours weep their burthen to the ground,
Man comes and tills the field and lies beneath,
And after many a summer dies the swan.
Me only cruel immortality
Consumes . . .

For Baudelaire death is not the enemy but captain of the ship:

O Mort, vieux capitaine, il est temps! Levons l'ancre!
Ce pays nous ennuie, ô Mort! Appareillons! . . .
Plonger au fond du gouffre, Enfer ou Ciel, qu'importe?
Au fond de l'inconnu pour trouver du nouveau!

O Death, old Captain, it is time, weigh anchor.
This country is a bore. O Death set sail . . .
Plunge to the bottom of the gulf — hell or heaven,
    who cares,
Just so we find the *new* in the depths of the unknown.

A century later T. S. Eliot takes his epigraph from Petronius, Arbiter of *le nouveau*, to Nero, Emperor of Ennui:

And when the boys would say to the Sibyl, "What is the matter?" she responded: "I yearn to die."

The *Waste Land* itself is a projection of the Sibyl's yearning:

What shall I do now? What shall I do?
. . . What shall we do tomorrow?
What shall we ever do?

Flaubert had taken boredom as his major theme also. It is not love or imagination or any idea that drives Emma Bovary from one novelty to another, but sheer disgust with whatever it is that she has. Again, a century later, Joyce captures the mood in his *Ulysses*, which is itself, as Frank O'Connor said in a capital and obvious phrase, "A crashing bore." Ezra Pound in approbation called it a second *Bouvard et Pécuchet*, that bible of the bored, the documentation of Flaubert's own consistent conviction that the whole of human life is inane. Molly Bloom says, "Yes I said yes yes yes . . ." But to what?

Lest we dismiss this as mere accident or pose, we must fix its cause — which is hatred of life and a commitment to the radical impossibility of significance. "It is strange how I was born with little faith in happiness," Flaubert wrote.

> When I was very young I had a complete presentiment of life. It was like a nauseous smell of cooking escaping from a vent. You don't need to eat it to know that it will make you sick.

A century later Sartre's book is titled *Nausée*, the experience of which he takes to be the ground of all philosophy — instead of Being, vomit. What is called "realism" in literature comes from the belief that beauty, truth, and goodness are illusions, or mere hypocritical posturings, that the real is the ugly, false, and evil. Much more than his book *Madame Bovary* is illuminated, if that is the word, by the following sentence Flaubert wrote to a friend:

> The loveliest of women is not very lovely on a dissecting table, with her intestines on her nose, one leg skinned and half a burnt-out cigar lying on her foot.

That terrible cigar distinguishes Flaubert's wit from his duller imitators; *Madame Bovary* is not a bore, nor is *Bouvard et Pécuchet*, but boredom is its origin and consequence.

Speaking of the poet and the reader both, Baudelaire states the case even more clearly. The poet — "prophet," superman of a new dispensation — he praises as ugly, evil, and disgusting, and then reveals his name:

> *Il en est un plus laid, plus méchant, plus immonde!*
> *Quoiqu'il ne pousse ni grands gestes ni grands cris,*
> *Il ferait volontiers de la terre un débris*
> *et dans un bâillement avalerait le monde;*
> *C'est l'Ennui! — l'oeil chargé d'un pleur involontaire,*
> *Il rêve d'échafauds en fumant son houka.*
> *Tu le connais, lecteur, ce monstre délicat,*
> *— Hypocrite lecteur, mon semblable, mon frère!*

40

There is another more ugly, more wicked, more
  disgusting!
Although he produces neither great gestures nor cries
He would gladly make the earth into garbage
And swallow up the world in a yawn.
He is Ennui — his eye charged with an involuntary tear,
He dreams of guillotines while smoking his hookah.
You know him, reader, this delicate monster,
— Hypocrite, reader, my double, my brother!

Eliot quotes the last line in *The Waste Land*.

  Monsieur Ennui is not his Neoclassic or Romantic brothers Messrs. Skeptic and Despair. The word "ennui" derives from the Latin *in odium* from a root meaning at once "to hate" and "to stink." Modernistic boredom is not the exhaustion that follows upon excess like Byron's; it is a positive disgust, and finally a hatred of existence itself. To Modernists the world is not an accident, as science led the men of the Enlightenment to believe and the men of the Romantic age to despair. The world is rather a deliberate, malicious, and very dirty trick. Everything that is, is wrong, and the only salvation is destruction. "Destruction was my Beatrice," said Mallarmé. Marx wrote:

Christian love is an obstacle to the development of the
revolution. Down with love of one's neighbor. What we
need is hatred. We must know how to hate; only then shall
we conquer the universe.

In his last years, Yeats was inspired by helpless rage:

Why should I seek for love or study it?
It is of God and passes human wit.
I study hatred with great diligence,
For that's a passion in my own control.

  The Neoclassicists believed that significance derived from reason. The Romantics attacked them, declaring that significance derived from the affections. Modernists attack them both, repudiating both reason and affection, repudiating the idea of significance itself. On the one hand, the ennui of the Neoclassic age was skepticism, the disgust that follows upon an exhaustion of the intellect. The great and meaningful disgust of Gulliver, awful as it is, is the result of a comparison between what he thinks ought to be and what he thinks is. Swift may have lost his reason, but he lost it between two real alternatives. On the other hand, the profound and moving ennui of the Romantic age was the result of an emotional saturation: Coleridge suffered from an overdose of Wordsworth.

> A grief without a pang, void, dark and drear . . .

Neoclassic ennui followed a failure of reason; Romantic ennui followed a failure of affection. But modern ennui is integral. It consists of a repudiation of what is generically and specifically human — both reason and feeling — reducing man to a physiochemical reactor, a confused and wretched vibration in a universe of particles and waves.

> For all that laugh, and all that weep
> And all that breathe, are one
> Slight ripple on the boundless deep
> That moves, and all is gone.

Tennyson understood perfectly what was about to happen, which was perhaps why he was not so cheery at the dawn — at least of this day. Darwin published the *Origin of Species* in 1859 and supplied a scientific theory to account for the monstrous Kraken. And as for love, Flaubert proposed it thus:

> We wretched little grains of dust, paltry vibrations of an immense movement, lost atoms ! — Let us join together our two nothingnesses in a common tremor, and let it be as endless as space.

And on another occasion:

> What is so very fine about the natural sciences is that they do not wish to prove anything . . . Human beings must be treated like mastodons and crocodiles; why get excited about the horn of the former or the jaw of the latter?

Display them, stuff them, bottle them, that's all — but appraise them or evaluate them: no! And who are you anyway, *petits crapauds?*[4]

A snarl like that is not the sneer of Neoclassic skepticism or the sad Romantic sigh. It says, "What did you expect? Existence is meaningless and hateful."

But why should anyone get into such a state of mind? The natural response of sense to sunlight and darkness alike is first and immediately delight. Pain is necessarily a secondary response as the privation of pleasure. Nausea — *à rebours* — is a reversal. The cause is neither literary nor broadly cultural, but narrowly philosophical, indeed epistemological: the assumption behind Modernistic ennui is that knowledge is of sensation only. The first and fatal step into the hermetic corridor is doubt. Doubt that the world exists and you have not begun to think philosophically for the first time, as Descartes imagined, you have rather entered the labyrinth of self from which there can be no escape except on waxen wings of a viewless poesy — art for art. At the center of the world of self the Kraken sleepeth; Yeats' rough beast begins to move his slow thighs and Mr. Kurtz, supping on a human tibia, lisps, "The horror! The horror!" Doubt that the world exists outside the self and there is certainly no way to prove that it does, since proof is "adequation of the mind" to such existence. Adequation to itself may be consistent, but then the mind can never assert anything outside itself. Bertrand Russell said the only man he ever met who understood him was Conrad.[5] Beneath the "upper deep" in Conrad's sea, beneath the surface action and the praise of sanity, is a crazy pessimism, as in Robert Frost, the blacker for the mask of reason, worse than the complaining of professional

---

[4]Quoted in Anthony Thorlby, *Gustave Flaubert and the Art of Realism.* There are innumerable remarks like this throughout Flaubert's *Correspondences.*

[5]Russell, *Portraits from Memory*, New York, 1956. " 'I have never been able to find in any man's book or in any man's talk anything convincing enough to stand up for a moment against my deep seated sense of fatality governing the world.' [Conrad] went on to say that although man has taken to flying 'he doesn't fly like an eagle, he flies like a beetle. And you must have noticed how ugly, ridiculous and fatuous is the flight of a beetle.' In these pessimistic remarks I felt that he was showing a deeper wisdom than I had shown."

pessimists like Hardy. "In the destructive element immerse."

This is the age of criticism. The poet, novelist, philosopher, and certainly the critic are, like Iago, "nothing if not critical." Their subject is the mind and not the world. Critical philosophy, Imagism, the psychological novel, the dominance of literary criticism and university research over the creative faculty are all results of mind bent back upon itself — regurgitated images, *nausée*, a literature of dogs who eat their vomit. But the one true food of music is delight in existence.

> When daisies pied and violets blue,
> And lady-smocks all silver white,
> And cuckoo-buds of yellow hue
> Do paint the meadows with delight . . .

In the life of the mind, as in all things, there is an order, having a beginning, a middle, and an end. Poetry begins in delight and ends in wonder; philosophy begins in wonder and ends in wisdom. Without the food of music, music sickens and love dies to leave suspicion and disgust. What Baudelaire, Flaubert, and even Frost and Conrad — despite their differences in other ways — what all the major writers of the century are sick of is themselves.

> *Le monde, monotone et petit, aujourd'hui,*
> *Hier, demain, toujours, nous fait voir notre*
>   *image . . .*
>
> The world, monotomous and small, today,
> yesterday, tomorrow, always, shows us our own
>   image . . .

cried Baudelaire. The prophet Tiresias in *The Waste Land* says:

> I have heard the key
> Turn in the door once and turn once only.
> We think of the key, each in his prison,
> Thinking of the key, each conscious of a prison.

In Eliot's notes to these lines we are referred first to a similar phrase in the *Inferno* spoken by Count Ugolino, who gnaws the skull of his eternally hated partner Ruggieri, locked forever in their common hatred as in life; when locked in a tower with his children, "fasting," as he puts it modestly, "had more power than grief . . ." Which means that he ate his own dead sons. The image is scarcely more terrible than the epistemology Eliot takes it to symbolize. That he thinks it is an epistemology is clear in the further reference in the notes to F. H. Bradley:

> My external sensations are no less private to myself than are my thoughts or my feelings. In either case my experience falls within my own circle, a circle closed on the outside; and with all its elements alike, every sphere is opaque to the others which surround it . . . . In brief, regarded as an existence in a soul, the whole world for each is peculiar and private to the soul.

The tower is oneself; one cannot get out. According to a famous definition, such a state of mind is Hell. "Hell is to suffer one's own will forever," said Boethius. And Dante added, "Abandon all hope, ye who enter here." There is no way out. However, Aristotle, in what one may confidently call the moment of truth in this perennial battle, saw that though there is no way out, there is no reason why anyone should go in the first place. This has all been argued out before against Heraclitus and the Sophists. Why doubt the existence of external reality? It is absurd to demand proof of what constitutes the only means of proof. The normal intellect like an eagle grasps in its beak the intelligible from the sensible and holds it. Concept comes from *capio*, "I seize." But the sensible is not a concept and cannot be captured. You taste the wine only so long as you keep the liquid on the tongue; taste cannot endure like an emotion or have a permanent validity like an idea. Anyone who rejects both abstractions and affections in the name of immediate experience inevitably must hold the world in disgust because sensations spoil, cannot be kept. The world of pure sensation disintegrates even as you experience it. Sensation is a Nessus shirt of fire, burning like a lust in which one must continuously seek the new out of a continuous and inevitable exasperation at one's failure. Descartes stepped through the sheets of flame into what seemed a pleasant limbo of philosophical doubt; but the heart of this hell is that ice where, locked in hatred forever, lie the treacherous spirits of total negation.

> Some say the world will end in fire;
> Some say ice.

At first sight the astonishing thing about Modern culture is that it goes on at all. But the astonishment is momentary too. Modern culture rushes on because it cannot stop. Ezra Pound, in *Make It New*, explains that the meaning of all his work and especially the *Cantos*, is "new-ism." He says that the Confucian doctrine of "process" will save the world, by which he means destroy the West. Process, as Pound describes it, is like the Marxist dialectic he hated, according to which nature and history are the outward appearances of an underlying warfare between interlocking opposites.

> The total process of nature . . . The process which unites
> outer and inner, object and subject, and thence constitutes
> a harmony.

Confucian "harmony," like Marxist "peace," involves the destruction of the opposites, which is to say — since nature is composed of them — all things. Such a doctrine is nihilistic. If you unite subject and object you destroy thought as Pound did sentences. "I hit the ball." But if "I" and "the ball" are one and the same, I have done nothing. In a universe of "process," prediction is impossible. In a novel or poem composed in such a language, lacking verbs, nothing happens, which is one of the reasons why they are such crashing bores. The *Cantos*, except for dazzling splashes here and there of sound and sight, make up another in a lengthening shelf of unreadable books of which *Finnegans Wake* is perhaps the most successful. And since the ultimate predicate is "is," such language destroys the idea of existence. "God," says Stephen Daedalus, according to his celebrated theory of "epiphanies," is a "shout in the street." God does not agree: "I am He Who is," He said. "In the beginning was the Verb." If you take verbs out of sentences you destroy thought; without the Verb, existence is illusion.

Having repudiated ideas, we are left with what we can immediately observe. Everything observable is indeed a process. Everything is seen, therefore, as motion; and since reason and affection cannot be seen, man is taken to be nothing more than motion also. It follows that the only existent is the "new" and the only time "now." By a parody of St. Augustine's intuition of God's eternal now, we ourselves are taken to be *tota simul*, the whole of reality in the present moment.

Anyone who conceives existence in this way is inevitably an exoticist. He allies himself with the current and the novel, and therefore always the strange. He has a rage for the latest thing because it would be death not to be new — the latest news, scientific invention, experimental novel, critical theory, fashion. To be is to be *avant garde*. Philip Spencer relates how on a trip to the then exotic Middle East, Flaubert and his friend DuCamp

> . . . met two Arab boats conveying slaves to Cairo; they were mostly women who had been stolen from the territory of Gallas, and the Arabs introduced among them a few old negresses to act as interpreters and proffer them some consolation. The two travelers went aboard and stayed as long as they could, haggling over ostrich feathers and an Abyssinian girl. Their purpose, said Flaubert, was to enjoy the *chic* of the spectacle.[6]

It is "to enjoy the *chic* of the spectacle" that we have been driven over and under the surface of the earth, savoring disease and slavery and worse. The exotic is the abnormal because the desire for the new derives from hatred of the norm. The latent force behind the tyranny of sex — in *Lady Chatterley's Lover, Corydon, Lolita* — is hatred, not only of courtship and married love, but of any love between men and women or men and men in friendship. Modern marriage, contradicted in its very pledge by the universal acceptance of divorce, really is a "legal cloak of prostitution." It was hatred of their mothers and of France that drove Flaubert, Rimbaud, and Gide to excursions in the Middle East and Africa. Hatred of "the old bitch gone in the teeth," as he called Ireland, drove Joyce to the ghettos of the emigrés; hatred of America and Jews drove Pound to Fascism and the asylum. One's country, like his knowledge, must be ground up to "make it

----

[6]Philip Spencer, *Flaubert: A biography*, London, 1952.

new," just as, according to the Marxist dialectic, "liquidate" is a word for synthesis. These exotic voyagers, especially the ones who have paraded as exiled artists, have thrilled sympathetic critics of the pipe-and-slippers set. But the artist has not been exiled. He has not even been treated with unprovoked hostility. Flaubert received every honor despite a lifetime of disrespect to his country. Joyce got money from the British government to live "in exile." Pound was honored by the Library of Congress while avoiding trial for treason. Treason is political exoticism, which explains the fascination Communism and Fascism have had for the intelligentsia. Sick of what they have — leisure and success — panting for sensations, they think defeat exotic and therefore cheer the other side. We can see them leaning out of windows like the decadent Roman ladies who were said to have thrilled at the entrance of the barbarian hordes, crying, "When do the rapes begin?"

The lust for the new, the exotic, is lust for the abnormal. It is against nature —*à rebours*, as Huysmans said; and that means that it is against human nature. It is bestial. The doctrine that knowledge is sensation drives the Modernist away from whatever he had and whatever he is. In order to renew the instantaneous sensation, he must flee whatever it is that he has — the bourgeois, the conventional — and he must flee the known and conventional past; in a word, he must flee civilization to seek the barbaric and the decadent. The modern Mount Parnassus is strangely situated. Leconte de Lisle, the Parnassian poet, having tired of the isles of Greece, scoured the world for barbaric and oriental sensations. Islam has fascinated modernists from Nerval to Gide, not because they were seriously interested in a foreign culture, but because Islam was to them not-Europe, and, being not-Europe, it was to them not-civilized, and, being not-civilized, it was a place where morals were not binding. The East has yet to be played out. Interest in yoga and Zen is so pervasive as to dumbfound the unwary into thinking that Kipling was wrong about East-West relations. He was not; it is merely that in calling for the suicide of Western civilization, some have discovered an extinction more thorough than any the West has so far conceived.

In the "Preface" to *Les fleurs du mal* Baudelaire wrote:

Though I have sung the mad pleasures of wine and opium,
I thirst only for a liquid unknown on earth, which the

48

pharmaceutics of heaven itself could not afford me; a liquor that contains neither vitality nor death, neither excitation nor extinction. To know nothing, to will nothing, to feel nothing.

The desire is not just for ordinary extinction, but for a consciousness of being extinct; not just to be ignorant, but to *know* nothing; not just not to feel, but to *feel* the acute sensation of absolutely nothing. As Baudelaire complains

> *Et mon esprit, toujours du vertige hanté,*
> *Jalouse du néant l'insensibilité.*
>
> My spirit, haunted by vertigo,
> Is jealous of the void's insensibility.

It is Being itself that the Modern wishes to destroy. The exotic is *ex-ontic* — outside Being. According to Mallarmé the purest poem is the blank sheet of paper —

> *le blanc souci de nos toiles . . .*

just as for the yogi the purest consciousness is precisely conciousness of nothing. What he calls *moksha*, or liberation, is absolute nonexistence. Buddha said:

> I say it is by destroying, stilling, stopping, renouncing, and abandoning all imaginings, all supposings, all thoughts of "I am the doer . . ." all latent "I am," that a Truth-finder is freed . . . . If material shape is impermanent, and if that which is impermanent is suffering, you cannot regard that which is impermanent, suffering and liable to change as: This is mine, I am this, this is my self. It is the same with feeling, perception (reason), and all consciousness, whether past, future, or present, subjective or objective, gross or subtle, mean or excellent, near or far — all must be seen as: This is not mine, I am not this, this is not my self.
> Herein monks, the latent bias "I am" is got rid of by the

monk, cut down to the roots, made as a palm-tree stump
that can come to no future existence.[7]

Every agent, Aristotle says, acts out of a desire for Being; whereas
Buddha teaches "desirelessness." For us, all things in the real world
naturally desire their own Being. For us, therefore, sensation is not
divorced from the reality that causes it, but rather, quite the contrary,
it is wedded to it by a marriage made in heaven and that ends in
"conception." It follows from the Realist point of view that man can
know, and knowing can love what he knows, that is, can desire it as
his and its good. Far from quenching, extinguishing, cutting himself
down to a dead stump, he flowers and seeds.

But we have been invaded by despair. A state of mind hitherto
considered morbid has become statistically — though not medically
or philosophically — the norm. The hell of Modernism is ennui — the
state of being conscious of not having sensations. Its heaven is having
acute sensations of nothing. And that is why the ultimate Modernist
poem is a blank sheet of paper, the ultimate painting "white on
white," the ultimate music silence, the ultimate philosophy Buddhism. Phenomenalism is an elementary stage of such nihilism; the
psychology of process an elementary yoga. The final stage is *shunyata*,
the void. Buddha has ten thousand shifting faces, ten thousand chang-
ing names — but Buddha does not exist. If we seek God He will be
what He is always, everywhere, in Texas or Timbucktu. If we want
strange gods, we must worship idols.

There is one final consequence. The last cavern in the exotic hell —
beyond the "ultimate" — is terror. One might expect sheer emptiness;
but the void becomes a teeming dream,

> . . . *un cauchemar multiforme et sans trêve.*
> *J'ai peur du sommeil comme on a peur d'un grand trou,*
> *Tout plein de vague horreur, menant on ne sait où;*
> *Je ne vois qu'infinie par toutes les fenêtres . . . .*

> . . . a nightmare, multiform, without truce.
> I fear sleep as one fears a huge hole.

---

[7]Coomaraswamy and Horner, *The Living Thoughts of Gotama the Buddha*, London,
1948.

I see nothing but infinity through every window . . .
Full of vague horror, leading who knows where.

The Modernist imagining the Infinite sees nothing and panics; it is difficult for him to understand that others do not imagine *what* but *Who* and have not seen emptiness but a warm and loving plenitude. Alone in a mental construction called "empty space," the nightmares start —

> What dreams may come
> When we have shuffled off this mortal coil?

— the creeping monsters from *out there*, the sponges of millennial growth, enormous polypi. In the last pitiful pages of *Mon coeur mis à nu* Baudelaire records his beatific vision:

> I have cultivated my hysteria with enjoyment and terror.
> Now I have a continuous vertigo, and today, 22 January
> 1862, I have received a singular presentiment: I have felt
> pass over me the wind of the wing of imbecility.

It is indeed "bitter knowledge" that one gets from such travel as this. But as Aristotle said, and as over two thousand years of Western civilization have affirmed, according to the common consent of the vast majority, according to what is justly called the philosophy of common sense — there is no reason to go on the voyage in the first place. "Levons l'ancre!" the poet cries. "Anchors aweigh!" The philosopher replies, "All ashore who are going ashore."

4 The Real Absence

In his *Preface to Paradise Lost*, C. S. Lewis defended himself against the charge of bias by arguing that a Christian is the best explicator of an obviously Christian poem. After all, he said, "What would you not give to have a real live Epicurean at your elbow while reading Lucretius?" The argument is tempting but, I think, false. The principle of objectivity has about it a stubbornness not so easily dismissed. The only way to look at anything is from some point of view, but some points of view are better than others; and the best is not the closest but the truest. If the Christian suffers from a delusion about the nature of reality, he is the last one to consult about a Christian or any other kind of poem. If, for example, Freud is right, the correct point of view to take of Christianity is the psychoanalytic. If, on the contrary, Christianity is true, we should want *Paradise Lost* expounded by Professor Lewis; and Lucretius, psychoanalysis, and the *Bhagavad Gita* expounded by Professor Lewis as well.

Objectivity, if it is not a mere prejudice, implies that there is a proper point of view. Practically speaking, the academic community has made a bad choice; it has settled for a point of view far beneath the Christian, beneath Lucretius and the Epicureans, somewhere down by Julian Huxley.

If he sticks to his principles, the Christian should be best qualified to examine the subject of this present essay because, committed to truth, he seeks to understand exactly what is there with the widest vision and most sympathetic heart — supposing that his faith is not in vain; supposing that not everything he says is foolishness. The commonest point of view at universities is the "scientific," which, while objective and informed, excludes evidence not directly measurable and misses therefore the essence of this subject, which, if anything, is spiritual. It is the evidence of things unseen that shows us what is there or not.

If he sticks to his principles! Some of the most foolish books about Oriental thought have been written by Christians soft in their own doctrines who have found in Buddha their fond idea of Jesus as the kindly guru with a "reverence for life." Christianity has become increasingly materialistic since the Renaissance, so that many professing Christians have it confused with social panaceas. They await the coming of a secular messiah who will lead the world into a workable United Nations — to peace, prosperity, freedom from sickness, old age, and death. Such a view ill equips a man for understanding anything, certainly neither Christian nor Oriental thought. The greatest impediment to the journey east has been ignorance of where it is one starts.

There are three bad kinds of Occidental commentary on Oriental doctrine. The first is hostile, or at best patronizing, interpretation by scientific critics who chop the texts to fit their own systems and by so doing distort and even destroy the doctrines. Even the patient Orientalists who edit texts and gather facts must miss the meaning because, as the text always insists, the letter killeth and the spirit giveth light. But worse are those who go beyond the facts to gather them into some comprehensive system of their own, like Jung, for whom the *I Ching* is a useful tool in psychoanalytic therapy, along with alchemy, astrology, and the Catholic Church in some cases.

The second genre is neurotic experimentation by cultists who feed their fantasies on misinformation. These desperate persons act out of a mania for power and peace. Tormented by the demons of their century, whom they seek to befriend and manipulate, they work with ouija boards, haruspicate and scry, take up astrology and crystal balls, interpret dreams, practice ceremonial magic, join secret societies where they are led by charlatans to distorted forms of Oriental doctrine in various theosophies. They seek power by these means. One could seduce movie stars if he could put them in hypnotic trances; if one had a demon who would dictate, he could write a *Paradise Lost*. And they seek peace because they are tormented to exhaustion with anxieties. The arc of this demonic life is plain in Baudelaire or poor Rimbaud and their recent less gifted imitators in the "beatnik" movement — the infantile eroticism, the taking of drugs, the fascination with violence and death. We meet them in full

53

comic vigor in Chaucer's astrology student, calculating siderial seductions of the Carpenter's wife, and the leaden-faced Canon's Yeoman whose skin was yellowed by alchemical furnaces. We meet the type when it is too late in Dante's *Inferno*, where those who have committed sins against nature are punished along with usurers and sodomites — those who try to make fecund what is by nature sterile and sterile what is by nature fecund.

Oriental masters teach that unlicensed experimentation is not just dangerous — which is no argument against it to a courageous or desperate person, if he were to achieve the Absolute — but foolish, at best a waste of time when medical help is needed, especially if one begins to get astonishing results like apparent charismatic gifts, so often taken as success when, in fact, if anything, they are signs of disqualification. From the point of view of Christian prudence, one should not depart from the practices of his church; from the point of view of oriental prudence, one should do nothing without thorough preparation under a qualified teacher.

The third bad kind of commentary is ridiculous amiability, an adjunct of tourism, in which well-meaning sentimentalists, sometimes vaguely Christian, confuse the will with the intellect and therefore "ecumenism" with syncretism. They think that because we must love our enemies, everyone is our friend. This attitude gives rise to weak and foolish attempts at suburban yoga and worse to the sad and shocking death of poor Tom Merton in a Bombay bathtub when he might have stayed at home singing Gregorian Chant according to the strict observance of his rule.

I suppose one must add a fourth. From Benares to the Bronx, the entertainment industry — of which universities are increasingly a part — supplies any number of great gurus. College students swallow goldfish, march for civil rights, "streak," and practice varieties of "collegiate yoga" mixed with Marxism, the experimental novel, and the purification of Lake Erie.

The purpose of a serious Christian confrontation with authentic Oriental tradition is good controversy, which churns competing doctrines and separates the false to leave the glistering kernels of the truth, like butter. The informed, diligent, and faithful Christian clarifies his own beliefs and learns precisely what he must reject as the most serious assault ever made against them. Without rancor, but with insistence on those articles of the Creed that it is eternal death to deny, one may take Hindu or Buddhist thought as a brilliant challenge, beside which the Catholic-Protestant controversy is a family quarrel. In fact, the family may be brought together sooner than we think in the face of the current resurgence of this perennial heresy that has worn so many different faces from Gnosticism to Modernism. Or we may be brought together at our funeral! If Christendom is sick — and who would deny it now? — it may be that Oriental thought, like shock therapy, will bring us to the brink of extermination and activate our will to live.

The greatest impediment to understanding Oriental thought is our failure quite to comprehend our own. Authentic Christianity is, first, the incarnation of the spirit and, second, the inspiration of the flesh. Since the Renaissance, when materialist philosophy began again to occupy positions of political and ecclesiastical power for the first time since the conversion of Rome, we have increasingly forgotten what the spirit is; so that for us spiritual experience is somewhat in our childhood memories about which we feel sentimental, as if it were myth or fairy tale or symbol but not operative as a present reality. So religion is mythologized, having its foundation in something misunderstood as "mystical" experience, such as Blake or De la Mare makes poems of.

> Some one is always sitting there,
>   In the little green orchard;
>   Even when the sun is high,
>   In noon's unclouded sky,
>   And faintly droning goes
>   The bee from rose to rose,
> Some one in shadow is sitting there,
>   In the little green orchard.

And indeed someone is. One of the most powerful attractions in Oriental doctrines is something we have as well at home but too quickly grow out of and repress — the reality of spiritual presences. Carlyle described it trenchantly:

> To speak in the ancient dialect, we 'have forgotten God';
> — in the most modern dialect and very truth of the matter,
> we have taken up the Fact of this Universe as it is not. We

have quietly closed our eyes to the eternal substance of things, and opened them only to the Shows and Shams of things. We quietly believe this Universe to be intrinsically a great unintelligible Perhaps.

Contrasting this with real religion, he said:

> Religion [to the monks at St. Edmundsbury] is not a diseased self-introspection, an agonising inquiry; their duties are clear to them, the way of supreme good plain, indisputable, and they are traveling on it. Religion lies over them like an all-embracing heavenly canopy, like an atmosphere and life-element, which is not spoken of, which in all things is presupposed without speech.

Among ordinary working Christians, the spiritual element is inconspicuous by its presence. Nowadays we get self-consciously and deliberately "unreal" every once in a while in the hope that thereby we become more "spiritual." We do not see one and the same event as bathed in the natural and the supernatural at once. If we saw the events in Christ's life really happening, we should not so much be terrified, awestruck, or holy, as disappointed. They did not occur in cinerama; the Sermon on the Mount did not come forth stereophonically amplified. We have come to expect a spiritual, like an artistic, event to be greater than reality and; by the same process, have come to think reality a paltry thing.

Even in the baroque imagination of St. Ignatius we can see the change. In the *Spiritual Exercises* he suggests that by strict attention to composition of place we construct in our imaginations as precisely as possible the vivid archeological realities of the past event — so that, for example, in the miracle at Cana, we see as in a painting by Vermeer the wedding guests, the musicians, the jars of water all exactly as they were. In medieval literature we find the reverse. In the *Second Shepherd's Play,* for example, angels suddenly appear to ordinary, contemporary shepherds right out of the current experience of the audience; and Christ is born in an English manger here and now. This attitude accounts for the simultaneity of the past and present in medieval literature and art. It is not archeological naivete that makes Chaucer present Troilus as a fourteenth-century youth just like the

Squire in his Prologue to the *Canterbury Tales*. In poetry, as in meditation, the past was seen as present because its meaning was present. The past event is materially long since gone, but if it is anything, it is spiritually present right now.

Chaucer's Canterbury pilgrimage is an obvious case in point. All sorts of real people — Professor Manly identified most of them right out of the London directory of 1387 — are going on a trip to a real place that is at once material and spiritual. The Shrine at Canterbury exists in its concrete reality as a fact; one goes there, and to be cured of a physical disease. The unhappy cook will be cured of his horrid sore — the more happy his customers who like blancmange. Chaucer tells us at the start that men

> Longen for to goon on pilgrimages . . .
> The Holy Blissful Martyr for to seke
> That hem hath holpen when that they were seke.

We have at Canterbury a material place charged with an efficacious energy that cures toothache and concupiscence and puts us in the presence of God. In the *Second Nun's Tale* we are told that when the brutal executioner walks off, leaving St. Cecilia partially decapitated, the faithful come to soak up her blood in sheets:

> But half deed, with hir nekke ycorven there,
> He lefte hir lye, and on his wey is went.
> The Cristen folk, which that aboute hire were,
> With sheetës han the blood ful faire yhent.

Today most people find this sort of thing offensive. It smacks of superstition and fills us with disgust. We do not mind entertaining ourselves with the sight of blood — the cinema is wet with blood; nor are we disdainful of the idea of a spiritual experience, though the cinema is not so full of that. But a bloody spiritual experience moves us to incredulity and anger.

For the greater number of educated people, Christianity is not serious; it will not bear up under critical shock. We quit Christ with our marbles and take up adult things like cigarettes and logical positivism. And yet spirits are facts and Christ and the martyrs in imitation of him shed real blood. You can stumble over spiritual substances and slip in this blood, but neither Oriental nor Occidental religion will ever really make sense unless you include them. When a person begins to reflect on this, he looks for some book, some teaching or science that might throw light on it. It seldom occurs to him to consider Christian books or institutions because people no longer shed their blood for them and rather talk about improving society and combating prejudice. As for the Christian facts like Christmas, they do not seem real. Something like one's mother, they are embarrassing and nice — but you do not go to your mother with an adult intellectual problem and neither do you search for truth among pretty stories. And so, like St. Augustine fleeing Monica, you take the journey to the East.

Strictly speaking, no Oriental doctrine in any of its authentic forms is a religion or, indeed, a philosophy. [8] Religion, however you define it, is a kind of relation, whereas the Oriental masters teach a doctrine that purports to obliterate the distinction between subject and object so that there is nothing to relate. Philosophical metaphysics is the science of Being, while Oriental metaphysics concerns non-Being. Metaphysics means "beyond" or "higher than" physics, physics taken in its Greek sense as the general science of nature. Physical science, according to this distinction, though it deals with abstractions, always proceeds from experience. Of metaphysics one can have no "experience" at all; metaphysics is beyond nature, beyond motion and change and therefore beyond the experiencing powers, fastened as they are to a "dying animal."

For Aristotle, Universal Being is the proper subject of metaphysics — the one, unmoved principle of the physical world of motion and change whom, St. Thomas says, "we call God." The Hindu says that Being is itself a limiting term; "to be" is "to be something" and therefore subject to change. So he argues that Aristotle's Being is merely generalized physics. The Hindu reserves for metaphysics that which is beyond Being — not the One, but Zero. Exposition of this

[8]The only serious Occidental commentary on Oriental doctrine from the Oriental point of view is in the work of René Guénon and A. K. Coomaraswamy. Guénon's works have been collected in the series *Etudes traditionelles*, Paris (Gallimard). In English see especially, Coomaraswamy (with Horner), *The Living Thoughts of Gotama the Buddha*, London, 1948; and *Hinduism and Buddhism*, New York, n.d.; *Buddhism and the Gospel of Buddhism*, Bombay, 1958. Guénon, *The Reign of Quantity*, London, 1953; *Man and His Becoming according to the Vedanta*, New York, 1958.

metaphysics is impossible in human language because sentences have verbs and all verbs reduce to the copulative "to be." Hindu formulae therefore are not doctrinal definitions; they are symbolical expressions of a superontological reality instantly comprehended in peculiar states of intuition. Metaphysical knowledge in this sense — an esoteric gnosis — transcends the distinction of Being and non-Being. In any kind of knowledge the knower must be united with the known; it follows that since metaphysical knowledge is infinite, it can be known only in the mode of an infinite knowing power and such knowledge cannot be attained by any person because persons are finite — limited, not infinite. How then is such knowledge attained at all? It cannot be attained by any person; however, it is possible for a person to transcend his own *persona*, his individuality. In metaphysical realization one ceases to be himself; he becomes some other thing; he does not say "I understand," but "it is understood." And this is why Hindu metaphysics is beyond religion and philosophy, both of which depend upon a relation that holds between some subject and object.

According to Hindu teachers, metaphysical realization is the end of various disciplines deriving from primordial tradition of which the Hindu is the oldest and purest, whose symbolic formulae are found in the *Vedas* and the vast literature of amplification and commentary on them, and of which Buddhism and its branches are local manifestations, and to which Taoism is in filial relation also. This body of texts is useless — so many dead letters — without the vivifying power of initiation in which the psyche is made apt to receive the teaching. Vedic, or Hindu, tradition is a body of symbolic teaching, the purpose of which is to aid persons in realizing an "existence" beyond the difference between existence and nonexistence. Religion, according to this teaching, is idolatry, because it takes the symbol for what is symbolized. Brahma, Vishnu, and Shiva are not gods, but symbols of metaphysical principles. And the six *darshanas*, or disciplines, are not competing philosophic schools of thought or religious sects, but complementary points of view. Views of what?

Imagine, according to a Buddhist meditation, a gull at dawn, gliding just above the surface of a lake that mirrors the gray bird and the gray dawn so perfectly that nothing is distinguished except for a single line the bird's claw draws across the surface of the water. For a moment, if you look closely, the three objects appear, though as the

59

gaze grows weary they blend again and it is as if you had seen nothing.

Oriental tradition may be reduced to that line and its erasure. *Moksha*, the Hindu term for "freedom," means liberation from the mental habit of duality. The state of Being that we occupy as rational animals is exactly that state in which reality is conceived according to the Principle of Being, as explained by Aristotle — namely, that the first thing to be said about something is that it is; and its immediate corollary, the Law of Contradiction — namely, that since something is, it cannot at the same time and in the same way be what it is not. According to the principles of Being and Contradiction, the lake *is;* it is not the sky; the bird *is,* and therefore is neither of the other two. According to Oriental tradition this state that we inhabit is not the state of the universe, but only one of a multiplicity of points of view depending on the state of the viewer. Reality is comprehended only according to the mode of the comprehender. Man, since he operates in the mode of "existence," cannot understand anything beyond existence.

Granted certain gifts, however, given certain initiations, and having practiced certain disciplines, a man may, according to Oriental tradition, transcend his physical state of rational animality and realize a higher metaphysical order, taking that word to mean not only "beyond the physical," "beyond nature" and all things in motion, but "beyond existence." From this higher point of view, reality is seen under the aspect of *advaita* or "nonduality." In such a state, the rational is transcended and the comprehender sees all things as one. The Principles of Being and Contradiction are transcended so that the comprehender sees an identity between things hitherto thought different — the lake, the sky, the bird; more astonishing, the comprehender and the comprehended are the same. According to the Principle of Being, "something is." But from the point of view of nonduality, that statement is the result of an illusion; it is the first manifestation of *maya*, the illusion consequent upon the state of rational animality. To say that something is and that something is not, from the point of view of *advaita*, is to say the same thing. Reduced to the simplest formula: "*Is* is not." Chuang-tse in his garden wondered whether he was Chuang-tse contemplating a butterfly or a butterfly contemplating Chuang-tse; and once he wondered this, he must have wondered also if he were the garden contemplating them both, and *ad infinitum*. That is the Ariadne's thread, not out of, but into the labyrinthine way of Oriental thought, at the center of which sits the fabulous Minotaur, the exotic beast so many Western intellectuals, especially in the last hundred years, have sought.

All of the hundreds of Oriental schools and their Western imitators, each with its technique, are so many ways of *yoga* or "discipline" leading to the achievement of *moksha* — liberation from *maya*, the illusion of "is" — so as to achieve the Supreme Identity: "*Is* is not."

Some yogas begin with physical exercise, the purpose of which is to condition the body to the point of realization of its latent psychic modalities. One can enlarge the pores, aerate the flesh and bone, and finally enlarge the pores of Being itself and let the black light of nonduality fill up the interstices, like water in a sponge. If you practice long enough, under a teacher who has himself mastered the technique (and there are few qualified teachers), and with certain aptitudes that very few possess; with diligence, which may mean twenty years or more of painful, grotesque, sometimes disgusting, application; and, finally, with luck (the kind you need to win the longest shot) — with all that, this tradition will enroll you in its corporation and you will, they say, *know nothing*, that is, have the direct intuition of vacuity, though we must no longer say "you" because your personality will not have survived the process. Sentences contradict; they do not express the real nature of Supreme Identity. Identity is not, after all, an experience, and language is metaphor that disappears along with the other apparatus of existence — the illusion that something is. In Identity, the person disappears.

Perhaps the most disconcerting aspect of Oriental tradition is its radical impersonalism. *Moksha* is liberation from one's self — not from selfishness as in Christian humility, but from the self itself; in the state of nonduality there is no distinction between one's self and any other self, or any other thing, or even nothing.

> A blanker whiteness of benighted snow
> With no expression, nothing to express.

The first stage in achieving the Supreme Identity is a kind of coagulation, such as cells achieve in the formation of tissue, in which persons become part of a collectivity. This is the famous *nous* of various gnosticisms; the "oversoul" of Emerson; the "cosmic consciousness" of Whitman's guru J. D. Buck; the "collective unconscious" of Jung. The neognostic Teilhard de Chardin mixes the idea with Marxism in his esoteric fantasies as a stage in the achievement of "Christ," who is no longer Jesus of Nazareth who died on a cross but the alchemical and occultist *Maximus Homo* or Superman that his evolutionary optimism says the whole human race is becoming. When psychologists describe the modern crisis in identity, they see as pathological what the yogi calls an elementary advance toward freedom.

Some yogas are physical, some artistic. For example, pictorial representation in Mahayana Buddhism is not illustration or decoration; images are contemplated with the same precision as postures are practiced in physical yoga and for the same purpose — the realization that contradictories are identical and especially that the mind is an impediment, that rationality prevents understanding. The purpose of imagining the gull at dawn is precisely that the one who contemplates that image will have the fluctuating sensation of both existence and nonexistence. He will hold in his vision an image of the state of mind he ultimately hopes to achieve permanently without the need of images.

Once this state of liberation from his "self" and from "the ten thousand things," as the physical universe is called, is achieved, there is discovered — one cannot say "he discovers" — an abyss beyond even emptiness because the masters of this tradition say that "nothing" is an illusion too. The ultimate irony is that after a lifetime of seeking, one discovers that there is literally nothing to have sought; not even "nothing," which is a rational idea. The word "person" derives from *persona*, meaning "mask"; the yogi at the end of the process puts his personality back on and acts out the play of existence. The word "illusion" derives from *ludo* meaning "I play," as one acts in a drama or takes part in a game. The most serious — and ludicrous — loss of identity beyond the elementary stages of not knowing who I am is the one in which I play that I am myself, one in which I become the Confidence Man or Fool — because I am not really myself at all.

It is often said that we all worship the same God in different ways, so that, as the world grows wise and tolerant, we shall all be friends together. Many today conceive the word *ecumenical* to mean a transcendent unity in which our differences, about which we have argued and even shed blood, will at last be erased, and the Buddhist will sit down with the Christian and the Moslem with the Jew — not just under the protection of a truce by which we promise to love one another though we differ, but under the final realization that we are not really different.

As a matter of fact, Oriental tradition has always proposed such a transcendental ecumenism. Throughout history, the only one *opposed* to such a view has been the God Who insisted by His very first commandment, "I am the Lord thy God; thou shalt have no strange gods before me." Gods, according to Oriental tradition, are so many images to use in meditation. They are like physical postures or statues made of *ghee*. They are supports for the difficult work of metaphysical realization. Once we accept this, the Hindu says, there can be no warfare or even disagreement, except of the amiable kind in which some are on one team, others on another. There is a Christian side, a Buddhist side, a thousand other sides, each leading to final liberation from the tyranny of difference. We are not just all brothers under the skin; we are really all under the same skin, exactly the same person — and so is God. The doctrine of the Mystical Body of Christ, the Hindu says, is misunderstood by Christians who think that somehow one's personal identity survives baptism. When you take on the New Man, the Hindu says, you have been ritually initiated into Oneness. "Atonement" is "at-one-ment."

A priest who claims to represent the mind of the American Church on the subject — which is impossible — recently invoked this mistaken kind of ecumenism, announcing at a press conference that theologians had worked out a "double-covenant theory" under which Jews could keep the old and gentiles follow the new. If this were true, St. Paul would have been as good before as after his conversion; and St. Stephen, when he was stoned, instead of praying for Saul of Tarsus, must have winked. In fact, Christ on the cross must have winked. In fact, according to a theology in which everyone who sincerely seeks the truth is said to receive the Baptism of Desire, the whole of Christianity is reduced to an awful, knowing wink — which is just what the Hindu says. The Christian missionary who invades the Orient with what Coomaraswamy calls "proselytizing frenzy" is thus criticized for not understanding the teaching of his own first yogi. Christ, they say, merely introduced another symbolism into the vocabulary of primordial tradition, added another set of icons to the lengthening shelf. The pity is that Christians took their symbols for facts and got themselves needlessly martyred by emperors who had no more relish for the job than Pontius Pilate.

The Oriental interpretation is as old as Christianity and as new as the latest ecumenical magazine. St. Peter confronted Simon Magus, who held the view. According to the vivid description in the Book of Acts:

> And when Simon saw that through laying on of the apostles' hands the Holy Ghost was given, he offered them money, saying, Give me also this power, that on whomsoever I lay hands, he may receive the Holy Ghost.

But the gift of God is purchased only by Christ's blood and is distributed only in His name.

> There is no other name under heaven, given among men, whereby we must be saved.

We cannot be saved by Moses, or by the Spirit of the Rainbow, or by Shiva. Baptism of Desire has been illustrated classically by the case of Valentinian. St. Thomas cites it from St. Ambrose:

> Hence Ambrose says of Valentinian, who died while yet a catechumen: I lost him whom I was to regenerate: but he did not lose the grace he prayed for.

Instructed, having made the commitment, Valentinian was simply waiting for the appointed day in the Church calendar when catechumens were traditionally baptized. He was not "seeking truth," or following the truth "as he saw it," but following the truth as it was explicitly taught by the Church. There are also those who in "invincible ignorance" fail in actual baptism through no fault, while believing in the God who will save them, and who therefore may be said to have received baptism virtually by desire. But these can scarcely be generalized into a theory of universal election, since very little ignorance is invincible, but rather "inexcusable," according to St. Paul:

> For the invisible things of him from the creation of the world are clearly seen, being understood by the things that are made, even his eternal power and Godhead; so that they are without excuse.

When God appears in the burning bush, He does not say, "I seem that

64

I seem"; rather the whole of Christian theology is fixed upon the fact that He is "He Who is." Because it is rooted in duality, the Christian tradition is opposed to the Oriental. There is nothing and there is something; and they are not the same. To say that God is a symbol is to deny the First Commandment. The Christian must reply to all varieties of transcendental universalism, though it may seem arrogant: "No. We do not worship the same God, you in your way, I in mine. I worship the one true God and you worship idols — you admittedly, because you say all gods are symbols. And indeed they are — all gods but mine." If like any normal man, having reason, you know from the things that are made the eternal power and Godhead, and still reject Him, you are without excuse and you will follow the way of everyone who has ever gone before you on that route.

> They are without excuse: Because that, when they knew God, they glorified him not as God, neither were thankful; but became vain in their imaginations, and their foolish heart was darkened . . . Wherefore God also gave them up to uncleanness through the lusts of their own hearts to dishonor their own bodies between themselves: Who changed the truth of God into a lie, and worshipped and served the creature more than the Creator.

The whole passage in the Epistle to the Romans describes the *modern* world both East and West, which is to say the world as it always is without God.

We have come down to this confrontation many times in history. Trajan made the same suggestion: "Put your God in the Pantheon along with the others." When the Christians replied, "There are no others," they were put to death for disrupting the civic order. The Christian says, "God really exists." In this inescapable fact, the whole fabric of pagan and oriental illusionism and the syncretism of religions that follows from it is dissolved. If God exists and really acts, and if one of His acts is creation, then the world really exists. Gull and lake and sky are not the same and are not illusions, though there are times such as dawn or dusk when several real events happen together and make things confusing; and there are times when we get tired or sick or drunk — there are twilights and vertigos. The long, deliberate *dérèglement de tous les sens*, as Rimbaud described the yoga he practiced — that derangement of the senses that all yogas produce — gives its practitioner the delusion of identity. If it is persisted in, it will wreck his mind so that indeed he will "know nothing." The Christian says that *moksha* is supreme insanity.

Let no one underestimate this old enemy who has done so much indirect service to Christendom, or disrespect his intellectual prowess. His attack has thrown down a moral challenge in every age. Christianity, like everything when it succeeds, grows fat, falters, almost fails until — unlike other things — it gets hold of itself again because Christ promised to stay with it until the end. At that next to last stage, when it is failing most, the symptom at once of its potential ruin and its imminent renewal is always Orientalism, under its various names. A raw and hungry asceticism cannot fail to appeal to a courageous youth, while a terrified, fat Christianity toadies to the enemy in think tanks and university symposia, shakes hands with sentimental assassins, gives the reechy kiss of peace to Communists and movie stars at revolutionary rallies publicized in magazines and television shows — like a rat running *onto* a sinking ship, it joins the dying modern world. There must be some other way — some other place — something more than cowardice and selfishness, something one can subject himself to without shame, something noble, beautiful, good, and true. It is a terrible but understandable mistake that the inexperienced and bursting heart, turning in disgust against the culture of the Golden Calf, confuses it with Christianity — because Christianity is certainly confused with it. And so we have the reason why some of the best have made the journey to the East. What they discover there at least is spirit.

Christianity nowadays is so immersed in worldliness that one scarcely sees its origins; the clergy preach sociology from the pulpit and monks have swimming pools. Earnest youth, though skeptical, admit to disappointment when they see the well-appointed mansions of a pharasaical asceticism — they want somebody, even somebody they disdain, not to be a hypocrite. Though they themselves might not believe, they hope someone does. It is no wonder that the seekers after social justice admire Che Guevara riddled with bullets in the jungle. He died for what he believed. You can see blood there; and the seeker after truth goes East where he finds a sacrifice of self, and having found it, knows that happiness can be found nowhere else. There is no other road to the true, the beautiful, and the good except renunciation, free from cant — through blood and the spirit.

But Oriental unworldliness — though it is genuine — overshoots the mark. It renounces God. The yogi wants to strip himself of all the accidental incrustations of the world. And he gets drunk on renunciation — just as the revolutionist gets drunk on blood.

The Oriental mystic gives up his house, his clothes, his friends, his family, his body, his mind, his soul, and God. He gives up Being and he misses what he seeks by infinitely more in excess than we have ever fallen short. Chesterton gives a figure for his own Oriental excursion in the story of the man who set out for Asia in a boat and was at last washed up on the shores of his heart's desire to find it all somehow tawdry and familiar like his childhood, until he realized he had turned around by accident and washed up on the beach at Brighton. The journey to the East — if undertaken honestly — will end where it did two thousand years ago, with the Magi going west to the stable in Bethlehem, falling on their knees, rapt in adoration before the real presence of Him Who is, born of a Virgin, made flesh and therefore in the world, to redeem the world not annihilate it.

Like radical politics, the theoretical study of Hindu doctrine may throw Christianity into the right perspective, may drive it back to its own spiritual roots, ashamed of its fat worldliness. The Christian who studies Hindu doctrine will discover that God is spirit and will learn as a certainty that he can never be satisfied with anything less. What he must learn by not only the study but the practice of Christian doctrine is the greater truth, that he will never be satisfied with anything more — anything less like social or political panaceas; anything more like the total loss of himself and God.

The answer to worldliness is to love the world as God so loved the world that He gave His only begotten Son to redeem it. The sin of worldliness is not love of the world, but the mistaken view that the world is all there is. Worldliness is to forget that things are creatures — not illusions but creatures created by God for the purpose of getting us to heaven. The Hindu is mistaken in thinking that the universal is greater than the particular. The final rest of the intellect, as of the will — of thought as of love — is in a person. To want more than God is to want infinitely less than He is. They fall upon their knees to adore the Real Absence.

Civilizations have their seasons. Oriental doctrine is like a garden gone to seed. The air is still, late dahlias drop their heads amid the pungent odor of decay; there is a peace here, certainly, a generosity of dissolution, a beauty so intense sometimes that it is itself a meditation. And that drowsy numbness that Keats, the autumnal English poet, celebrates comes over us together with a longing so heavy the heart breaks.

Because the West has reached its fall, we find the Oriental doctrines truer than our own; they represent more honestly the way things seem now. Summer has become an illusion — Indian Summer we call it now. Beautiful, but unreal. And all this dying life seems but a preparation for some funeral. There is a delicious sadness that comes over us — felt in Keats; raised to its highest power in the still, sad music of Tennyson; classical and cool in Matthew Arnold; bitter in Thomas Hardy; cold in Robert Frost; dry as stalks in T. S. Eliot, at the end of whose most influential poem occurs, as he says in a celebrated note, "the formal ending of an Upanishad"—*Shanti shanti shanti*, the "peace which passeth understanding." It is certainly true that for many (not all, but for a significant number, perhaps of a certain type, and most likely at certain periods in history) the only way to Christianity is, as Eliot said, "by the back door." For them this Oriental vision, by antithesis, is a kind of Advent, a season of spiritual preparation. It was so with Eliot himself, it was so at the end of the pagan world with St. Augustine. It was so in fact with the whole of the pagan world; and it may be so for us today, and for the East itself today in its flagrant bitterness, the stirrings of new life, a vehement April.

Controversies churn. According to a Hindu myth, history is a butter churn, turned by delightful, mysterious girls who just when they think things are hopeless and their arms and wrists grow tired — are about to get some butter.

5 The Emperor's New Literature

Human as well as physical nature abhors a vacuum. There is a universal need for humanistic learning, and if it is withdrawn, a surrogate moves in to take its place. When the Greek and Latin classics that formed the core of our culture until the twentieth century were removed, the various national literatures replaced them. Matthew Arnold was appointed to the first chair in English literature at Oxford in 1857, the first time a major university assented to the teaching of a literature other than the classical. It forms a watershed in our culture; from 1857 on, we took the downward slope. A hundred years later we see how the classics have materially disappeared from life, though they maintain a formal presence in our schools. Classical culture is at the last ditch — why?

In 1882 Matthew Arnold delivered a famous lecture from his chair at Oxford, which begins with a quotation from King Solomon and goes on to apply its wisdom to the state of education at that time:

> "No wisdom, nor counsel, nor understanding against the Eternal," says the Wise Man. Against the natural and appointed course of things there is no contending . . . . To deprive letters of the too great place they had hitherto filled in men's estimation and to substitute other studies for them [is] now the object of a sort of crusade . . . . Sir Josiah Mason founds a college at Birmingham to exclude "mere literary instruction and education"; the *Times* . . . thinks that a hundred years hence there will only be a few eccentrics reading letters and almost everyone will be studying the natural sciences.

Well, Sir Josiah and the *Times* have won; and, while it is pejorative to call them eccentrics, today indeed Greek and Latin are read by a few while almost everyone studies, more or less, the natural sciences.

Yet whatever may be said for the natural sciences — and we all agree it is a great deal — they are not humane letters. Letters had "too great a place" in our estimation once, and we are justly proud of the gains in technical studies since the nineteenth century. But do we want to go so far as to have a merely technical civilization? A hundred years after the great revolution in our culture, we might question the "too great place" of science. So many are shocked today to find their children lacking religious motivations, lacking patriotism, lacking even a very clear sense of moral responsibility. They fail to realize that these virtues are in great part culturally determined. We have lived on cultural capital from a past generation, having failed to counteract depletion. In the late nineteenth century the past was junked and in the twentieth we have reaped the wind.

George Gissing, in a remarkable and largely overlooked novel published in 1891, called *New Grub Street*, prophetically satirizes the triumph of the new ignorance:

> Jasper changed the topic of conversation, and presently Whelpdale was able to talk with more calmness. The young man, since his association with Fleet and Co., had become fertile in suggestions of literary enterprize, and at present he was occupied with a project of special hopefulness.
>
> "I want to find a capitalist," he said, "who will get possession of that paper *Chat*, and transform it according to an idea I have in my head . . . ."
>
> "The paper is rubbish," remarked Jasper . . . . "Precisely, but the rubbish is capable of being made a very valuable article . . . . In the first place, I should slightly alter the name; only slightly, but that little alteration would in itself have an enormous effect. Instead of *Chat*, I should call it *Chit-Chat*!"
>
> Jasper exploded with mirth.
>
> "That's brilliant!" he cried. "A stroke of genius!"
>
> "Are you serious? Or are you making fun of me? I believe it *is* a stroke of genius. *Chat* doesn't attract anyone,

but *Chit-Chat* would sell like hot cakes, as they say in America. I know I'm right; laugh as you will . . . . Now do let me go on," implored the man of projects when the noise subsided. "That's only one change, though a most important one. What I next propose is this . . . No article in the paper is to measure more than two inches in length and every inch must be broken into at least two paragraphs."

"Superb!"

"But you are joking, Mr. Whelpdale!" exclaimed Dora.

"No, I am perfectly serious. Let me explain my principle. I would have the paper address itself to the quarter-educated; that is to say, the great new generation that is being turned out by the Board schools, the young men and women who can just read, but are incapable of sustained attention. People of this kind want something to occupy them in trains and on buses and trams . . . . What they want is the lightest and frothiest of chit-chatty information — bits of stories, bits of description, bits of scandal, bits of jokes, bits of statistics, bits of foolery. Am I not right? Everything must be very short, two inches at the most; their attention can't sustain itself beyond two inches. Even chat is too solid for them; they want chit-chat."

Jasper had begun to listen seriously.

Fix these two quotations in the memory, the one from Matthew Arnold's lecture "Literature and Science," the other from George Gissing's novel *New Grub Street:* Sir Josiah Mason founds a college at Birmingham to exclude "mere literary instruction and education," and Whelpdale says, "I would have the paper address itself to the quarter-educated . . . the great new generation that is being turned out by the Board schools . . . young men and women who can just read, but are incapable of sustained attention." Whereas for two thousand years we have had a real culture known by many or by few according to the ups and downs of politics, today we have a pseudo-culture known by all. We are all quarter-educated.

Literature is the ox of culture, its beast of burden. Without it we have no means of bearing culture. Nowadays we all suffer shamefully from a narrow shallowness that leaves us prey to the first fraud outside the margins of our specialty who, bristling with foreign phrases and widely scattered showers of exotic imagery, presents himself as the new deluge — and there you have on the ruin of real culture the triumph of ignorance, the new barbarism presenting itself under the aegis of the encyclopedic confidence man who fools most of the people most of the time and very often, surrounded by foolish flatterers, fools himself, thereby adding an appalling sincerity to the general slide.

James Joyce was not himself quarter-educated; he was half-educated. He was sent to Jesuit schools in Dublin around the turn of the century, and in this provincial city and among that order, the reforms of Sir Josiah had not yet arrived. The college Joyce attended had been founded by Newman, whose lectures on the aims and principles of the new venture constitute *The Idea of a University*. Newman failed as a college administrator because he was too serious, and the school was taken over by the more experienced and practical Jesuit order shortly after his tenure. One of its distinguished professors was Gerard Manly Hopkins, the poet, who taught Greek composition — students at the age of sixteen, equivalent to our high school juniors, wrote compositions in the ancient Greek language; perhaps not very good ones, but in Greek. Though Hopkins had died by the time Joyce entered, and the level had gone down, it had not sunk so far as in more up-to-date establishments in England and especially in America. Joyce learned small Latin and less Greek; he lacked the learning of a fully educated man of letters like Arnold, Ruskin, Newman, or Hopkins, but, compared with the American emigrés he lived among in Paris, he was omniscient. He found himself above a world that, according to the natural and appointed course of things against which there is no contending, had degenerated to the quarter-educated clientele of Whelpdale's *Chit-Chat*.

Joyce began his literary career in Paris with some fairly good imitations of the latest literary vogue of Chekhov and Turgenev. The result is a collection of sketches called *Dubliners* that legitimately takes its place, rather quietly, in our minor literature. But Joyce was more ambitious. In imitation of Flaubert he rewrote a juvenile novel he had half-consigned to the flames — the carefully singed manuscript is now in one of our university libraries. The result was *Portrait of the Artist as a Young Man*. Sophomoric theologizing and Flaubertian methodology

72

— but without the mordant wit — spoil whatever charm the matter might have had. It is a cold book. It has become a standard text in college literature courses because, written to formulas, it illustrates them nicely; it has an air of erudition; and chiefly because, tickling the rebellious sentiments of graduate assistants, it is at once teachable and seditious, excellent material for those who would immerse themselves and their students in the destructive element. Stephen Daedalus, the hero, betrays his church, his country, his father, his mother, his friends, swearing allegience to himself as Superman, the Artist, who is taken to be an emergent species bearing the same relation to his fellow men as Adam to the apes.

According to one of many books on Joyce, "It is hardly necessary to prove *Ulysses* a masterpiece of modern literature."[9] This critical study — a fair sample of its kind and against which I have no animus, but must choose one to make example of — begins with a quotation from someone whose identity is momentarily withheld for rhetorical effect:

> "Filthy in word, filthy in thought, furious, raging, obscene" — how often these and similar charges have been levelled at Joyce's *Ulysses!* But it is not a modern critic from whom these words are quoted, nor is it Joyce who is being attacked; it is Thackeray misjudging the greatest satirist in the annals of English literature — Jonathan Swift!

Note, (1) the false logic. Joyce and Swift are both accused of the same crime. Swift was innocent. Therefore Joyce is innocent. By reasoning like this, all men ever accused of any crime would be innocent if one among them was — innocence by association. (2) A point of fact. Thackeray did not misjudge Swift. Out of his large, strong, and generous mind Thackeray understands, appreciates, and then severely judges him. He is speaking of *Gulliver's Travels:*

> As for the humour and conduct of this famous fable, I suppose there is no person who reads but must admire; as for the moral, I think it horrible, shameful, unmanly,

---

[9]Richard Kain, *Fabulous Voyager: James Joyce's Ulysses*, Chicago, 1947.

blasphemous; and giant and great as this Dean is, I say we should hoot him. Some of this audience mayn't have read the last part of *Gulliver*, and to such I would recall the advice of the venerable Mr. Punch to persons about to marry, and say "don't." When Gulliver first lands among the Yahoos, the naked, howling wretches clamber up trees and assault him, and he describes himself as "almost stifled with the filth which fell about him." The writer of the fourth part of *Gulliver's Travels* is like the hero himself in this instance. It is Yahoo language: a monster gibbering shrieks and gnashing imprecations against mankind — tearing down all shreds of modesty, past all sense of manliness and shame; filthy in word, filthy in thought, furious, raging, obscene.

And dreadful it is to think that Swift knew the tendency of his creed — the fatal rocks towards which his logic desperately drifted. The last part of *Gulliver* is only a consequence of what has gone before; and the worthlessness of all mankind, the pettiness, cruelty, pride, imbecility, the general vanity, the foolish pretention, the mock greatness, the pompous dullness, the mean aims, the base successes — all these were present to him; it was with the din of these curses in his ears, that he began to write his dreadful allegory — of which the meaning is that man is utterly wicked, desperate, and imbecile, and his passions are so monstrous and his boasted powers so mean, that he is and deserves to be the slave of brutes, and ignorance is better than his vaunted reason. What had this man done? What secret remorse was rankling at his heart? What fever was boiling in him, that he should see all the world blood-shot? We view the world with our own eyes, each of us; and we make from within us the world we see. A weary heart gets no gladness out of sunshine; a selfish man is sceptical about friendship, as a man with no ear doesn't care for music. A frightful self-consciousness it must have been, which looked on mankind so darkly through those keen eyes of Swift.

That is Thackeray very keenly judging Swift. And note, (3) that

74

Joyce is nothing like Swift anyhow. Swift despised the human race because to his bloodshot eye the human race was hopelessly immoral. Joyce despised morality. The filth in Swift derived from his disgust, from the "savage indignation" that lacerated him and finally drove him mad — Swift used filthy language to denounce the filth he thought had ruined us. And, not incidentally, Swift's terrible imprecations are not even remotely comparable to Joyce's medically documented obscenities. The word "filthy" used by Thackeray judging Swift has only an analogical relation to the word when used on Joyce.

But our critic tries to make a case for Joyce as satirist:

> The earnestness and honesty of satirists, their clear-eyed vision of evil, their moral horror, have ever been subject to misinterpretation by tender-minded readers. The weapons of irony and indirection are double-edged and often return to wound the assailant as well as the victim. Since most twentieth-century authors use these weapons, it is not surprising to find that misguided zealots have accused modern literature of the very evils it attacks — licentiousness, social irresponsibility, perversion.

Again a point of fact, obscured by the technique of what is vulgarly but accurately called the smear. Readers who are repelled by Joyce are "tender-minded" and those who attack his work are "misguided zealots." Thackeray, himself a very great satirist, though a gentleman, was not tender-minded and certainly comprehended irony and indirection. Another question of fact. Is it true that twentieth-century authors attack the evils they describe? Does Henry Miller satirize licentiousness or Gide perversion?

But suddenly the wind has changed! A few pages later we are told that Leopold Bloom

> if not a great man by conventional reckoning . . . at least is great of heart, and he suffers greatly . . . . Neglected, despised, this wandering Jew carries in his soul the secret of love.

So Joyce is not like Swift at all. Far from "moral horror," he excites in his readers, apparently, a lyrical compassion. As a matter of fact, Morris Ernst, the civil rights lawyer, hailed the *Ulysses* case as magna charta in the struggle for the emancipation of sex. And note just in passing that the word "conventional" reduces morality to "common agreement"; by such a sliding use of words, moral law is converted into something made up as if by a convention, especially of bourgeois philistines, and applied tyranically to the rest of the human race and especially poor misjudged Leopold Bloom — "If not a great man by conventional reckoning," by what kind of reckoning then? Leopold Bloom's wife Molly is called

> a masterpiece of comic portrayal; comparison with Chaucer's Wife of Bath is inevitable. Both have a hearty animal-like acceptance of life in all its aspects. She shows no acquaintance with her literary predecessor, though it is probable that she would waste no love on her fifteenth-century rival.

Putting the Wife of Bath in the wrong century is not half so great an error as comparing the two at all. But if we are to have a warm-hearted sympathy for this lusty, life-loving twentieth-century Wife of Bath — overlooking the misinterpretation of Chaucer — what has become of the savage Swiftian?

Another critic writes in the same vein:

> *Ulysses* has a happy ending, like the *Divine Comedy*. Plainly moral in theme, *Ulysses* nonetheless is not plainly moral. No wonder that some readers, diverted by occasional indecencies and confusing decorum with virtue, find the book immoral . . . . For me, the significance of the form Joyce made is a humane and charitable understanding of mankind that makes me glad to be alive and part of it. Charity, for me, is the radiance of this great whole, this intricate harmony.[10]

As if the indecencies in *Ulysses* were really just occasional; as if

---

[10]W. Y. Tindall, *James Joyce,* New York, 1950.

adultery and perversion were simply "indecorous"; as if one were supposed to have charity for sin; as if a book that ostentatiously advocates disobedience to all ten commandments were moral in theme; as if it were humane to degrade the human body.

Joyce is called the "greatest master of English prose." "Ulysses is a world-book. The Divine Comedy of our age . . . . Not for nothing were Joyce's heroes Swift and Ibsen." But what is Swift to Dante or Ibsen to either? Joyce is favorably compared to Shakespeare, Homer, the list is endless — comparisons so reckless and contradictory are simply a desperate assault on the obvious. But how should subscribers to Whelpdale's *Chit-Chat* know the obvious?

> Humanism has been discredited, so often has it been used to defend reactionary politics, authoritarianism, and the economic status quo, while a vigorous naturalism and relativism in philosophy and literature seek a new basis for humane values . . . Marx, Darwin, Freud, Bergson and others agree in refuting the accepted faith in rationalism . . . Of the three major writers of the twentieth century — Marcel Proust . . . Thomas Mann . . . and James Joyce — Joyce appears to be the one who faced most unflinchingly the decadence of bourgeois society.

Sad jargon of the university Marxist who, in half-conscious masochism, advocates revolutionary overthrow of the civilization that has sheltered such men as himself and Joyce from their own destructive wills and from the natural desire of the ordinary redneck to eliminate them as he would a horsefly — the nihilists, the destroyers, those who rage against the light, thirsting for confusion and disorder.

"*Ulysses,*" our critic says, "is fun to read." But if ever a book was written not to be read at all, it is *Ulysses*. I know of no one — and I have been associated with professors of literature for thirty years — no one, not even members of the Joyce Society, or authors of books on Joyce, who has ever read *Ulysses*. You can read in and at it and certainly about it; certain passages have been put on phonograph records and been made into plays and movies. But read it you cannot. Check any library and you will see an indirect proof. Books about Joyce are thumbed to death; *Ulysses* itself, except for those atrocious passages appealing to the mentally ill and to curious adolescents — to which the book falls open from overuse — *Ulysses* itself remains untouched. "*Ulysses*," said Frank O'Connor, "is a crashing bore."

Put positively, what I mean is this: James Joyce's *Ulysses* is indeed the book of the century. Its phenomenal success is due to two cooperating causes in modern culture: (1) the triumph of ignorance — that loss of humanistic education that has reduced us to the quarter-educated, making us a prey to cultural confidence men; and (2) the fact that such confidence men indeed operate — the reputation of *Ulysses* being the direct result of an assault on common sense by a half-educated intelligentsia in the universities and quarterlies.

The Emperor has no clothes on. Confidence men have come to town, pretending to be tailors. They have made a suit of nothing for the Emperor to wear and the poor fool parades with absolutely nothing on. The crowd does not cry out because the clever frauds have spread the word: anyone who cannot see the silk and golden cloth is "tenderminded" and a "misguided zealot," a "bourgeois reactionary."

The theses and the books continue to come off the production lines, and the Joyce industry rides on confidently to its 1929 and perhaps in an age of Keynesian pump priming — who knows? — the Emperor can go naked for a long, cold, subsidized parade.

But all this still does not explain why the Emperor's New Literature has almost completely displaced the classics. What were the formal and final causes of this fantastic cultural enterprise? What formal disposition of the quarter-educated made them vulnerable? After all, a two-thousand-year-old religious and literary tradition could not so lightly be disposed of, even if we neither love nor understand it anymore. Though all the *avant-gardists* struggle to subvert it, one would think the classics would prevail, a while at least, by sheer inertia. They did not because we were disposed against them by an attitude towards change — a theory of history become habitual, which, as in judo wrestling, twists the force of the dominant mover against him. The formal cause of this surprising rout is the notion that change is virtue. And from this it follows, of course, that if the old is maintained by law, the new and therefore the good must be subversive. Joyce said, "Civilization was created by its outlaws." Homer? Aeschylus? Solon? Pericles? Caesar? But who cares for the facts? It is the slogan that wins. "The important thing about history," Marx said, "is not to understand it but to change it." History, according to this doctrine, is an instrument in the hands of the Party. If for its purposes the Party needs us to believe that civilization is the work of its outlaws, the Party will make it so.

Take for example those two most notorious old gunfighters, Socrates and Jesus Christ. Socrates is put to death for corrupting the young — a sort of ancient André Gide; and Christ, the Galilean Castro, bites half a burnt-out cigar. But Socrates denounced immorality as subversive to the state, advocated a hierarchical society with Egypt as its never-moving model for total preservation of tradition, refused to escape from jail, into which he had been thrust by a revolutionary government, and willfully accepted his execution because he did not want by his example to teach anyone to be an outlaw, even though he was innocent. As he put it, "I am the victim not of law but of men." Socrates did not die because he was immoral or because he ever advocated immorality or because he taught that the laws forbidding immoral behavior were wrong. He died because cruel, mistaken, vulgar, violent, rebellious men had seized state power through riots and "spontaneous" demonstrations, by stirring up every pot of malcontentment, instigating the young, the social misfits, the envious; and they succeeded in part because fifty years of philosophical relativism under the teaching of the Sophists had softened the brains and hearts of a whole generation. Socrates died because a clique of rebellious men, through naked power, were able to subvert the law.

And only professional anti-Christians could have manufactured the blasphemous idea of Christ the Communist. It takes a special kind of hatred to accuse of disobedience One who gave His life for its opposite. The whole point of Christianity is His innocence. Civilization is not the creation of its outlaws but of men who have worked hard in the sweat of their brows, building on the past — against the outlaws, the immoralists, the advocates of violence and death. In obedience to natural law and by the grace of God, a few good men have stemmed the blood-dimmed tide in every generation, though now it seems to some as if, at last, we were going under.

As it is politically with outlaws, so morally and psychologically. The heroes of the movement for the new will be the queer and the sick. In precisely the same year that Matthew Arnold assumed the chair of modern poetry at Oxford, Gustave Flaubert and Charles Baudelaire published *Madame Bovary* and *Les fleurs du mal*, the most influential novel and book of poems respectively of the whole of Modern literature. Baudelaire said, "Life is a hospital in which we are all dying of a deadly disease," and in a celebrated poem sang of a putrifying corpse in elegiac music reminiscent of Horace. Flaubert was excited by disgust. He collected notebooks full of what he called *sottises*, examples of nonsense from the newspapers, conversations overheard in trains, writings on the walls of washrooms. From his collection he projected a vast unreadable work, an interminable litany to the essential boredom of existence — the literature no longer of the bloodshot eye like Swift's, but of an eye grown yellow. His last and most ambitious work was to have been a book so stupid no one could ever read it. He died before its accomplishment. It remained for Joyce to achieve that *tour de farce* in *Finnegans Wake*.

Ulysses, well on the way to Flaubert's goal, purports to be an artistic experiment in which the author transcribes the details of a single day as actually experienced in the consciousness of representative figures. The "stream of consciousness" technique, as it is called, is an artistic error to begin with. Art, as Aristotle said, is not chronology but a "story" that presupposes intelligent selection according to a form conceived in the mind of the artist. But the book in reality only purports to be such an experiment; it is not a stream of consciousness but a montage of pasted clippings from the library like Eliot's *Waste Land* or Pound's *Cantos*. The laborious compilation of *sottises* is not merely the transcription of everything that passes through the consciousness of a few Dubliners on a day in 1916, but a selection of archetypical graffiti that by allusion is supposed to tell the story of Ulysses' return to Ithaca and, at the same time, perhaps, Dante's ascent to heaven and half a dozen other things.

When you turn to the book itself, having read the baffling Baedekers, none of this makes any difference anyway because you are struck immediately by the actual fact of total impenetrability. In many passages, word after word, according to whatever scheme you may want to read it, register no meaning except when they descend to obvious obscenity. If the book is meant to be a stream of consciousness in the minds of representative men, we should ask: Representative of what? For many years critics speculated on the reasons for the great amount of dull filth. As we have seen, it has been defended both as satire and as propaganda for the liberation of sex. But even on either of these grounds it was difficult to excuse the painstaking, obsessive, photographic quality of the detail, and the extravagance of the material. One might understand — without agreeing with it — the argument of Bertrand Russell that adultery is a private affair in which the state should take no interest; and it is possible to understand a satirist putting his characters up to such behavior in order to show how gross it is. But this is not what Joyce does. He does not make adultery either enticing or ridiculous, funny or even plausible. He shows in closeup detail a sadistic prostitute grinding lighted cigars into the rump of a masochistic ne'er-do-well who is supposed to be Ulysses. As they say in pornography trials, there is just no "redeeming literary merit" in this kind of thing.

And now we know the Cornell University Library has material from Joyce's private papers proving him to have been mentally ill, which adds to nihilism the guying of the sick. It is an offense against their dignity, against the rights of the sick, to exploit their illness even if, like Joyce, they themselves desire it. If *Ulysses* is the stream of Joyce's consciousness, it certainly should never have been published. This is not a matter of being tender-minded or zealous, but medically ethical. And when we turn from the consideration of the pathetic author to the rights of persons at large, we must consider the effect of such material. When people behave in real life as Joyce's characters do in the book, it is time to call the police and trust them to keep the names of the children out of the papers. Leopold Bloom, the hero of *Ulysses*, the man our critic called "great of heart," is what the newspapers call a "molester." But saying that, we shall now no longer be accused of tender-mindedness but of police brutality. Walking up the down escalator, we suddenly discover that Joyce is tender and *we* are the vicious satirist. Zealous? Yes, but not misguided. It must be put to the charge of publishers and teachers that this book has been outrageously promoted in high school classes as well as at college. For this they are guilty of more than bad taste. There is a direct cause and effect relation between reading of this kind and the loss of manliness and purity, and even the violation of self and others.

Is this to suggest that literature has moral force, that taste and behavior and the sense of truth and decency are influenced by books — that literature has consequences? If not, why should anyone ever have taken it seriously?

And yet, they say, what can you do? "Against the natural and appointed course of things there is no contending." Do the people who shrug their shoulders at this rubbish really mean to acquiesce? Do they really mean to say that they couldn't care less if their grandchildren become practicing perverts? Do they really mean to invite — while washing their hands of it — another age of Nero or King James? Every criticism is greeted with that ignorant and irrational shrug.

It is not reasonable to circulate pornography. That you cannot turn back the clock is no answer at all to the question of what time it is. That change is inevitable leaves us precisely with the question: What is the right thing to do? To say that the school boards in the late nineteenth century followed Sir Josiah Mason and his parvenu philosophy rather than the greatest men of letters of the age is not to say they had to; nor to say that today, now that we see what a mess we have made of education, we must continue to destroy culture. "No wisdom against the Eternal!" But Arnold adds, "To resign oneself too passively to the supposed designs of the Eternal is fatalism. Perhaps they are not really the designs of the Eternal at all, but designs, let us, for example, say, of Mr. Herbert Spencer."

Anyone who cares seriously about education will simply unplug the television set, burn most of his "Modern Library," learn at least some Latin and a little Greek, read the best vernacular literature, and, if he finds that he cannot make the effort or that having made it, it seems to bear no fruit, then he will be silent and defer to the judgment of his betters. The shameful state of culture can be improved as soon as we want to improve it — and that will not be by means of new teaching devices, publication schemes, and Morrison's Pills.

Ulysses is a severe symptom of a deadly disease in modern culture. The cure is to put ourselves under the causes of health. In the particular case of literature, these are primarily the Greek and Latin classics, and the classics of various national literatures of Europe written in imitation of them — which, indeed, make little sense in their absence — for English-speaking people, the Oxford Standard Authors. And this means the overthrow of a narrow fatalism that bleeds the past so that people are more ashamed of lacking the latest gadget or the latest issue of *Psychology Today* than the life of our civilization.

The restoration of health means these three things — and one thing more. From the point of view of literature alone, the remedies so far supplied would be enough. But it is a poor doctor who considers only the disease and not the patient. In literature classes at school we talk about plot, character, and form; we discuss the historical materials the author uses, what we call the "matter" or the content; and then, most difficult and rewarding of all, the author's intentions, which is the "theme." Theme is the motivation of the work that determines and pervades it. The theme of Joyce's work may be summed up in a single sentence, very well known, which the hero of both *Portrait of the Artist* and *Ulysses* quotes as his motto. It is taken from a notorious source: *Non serviam.* Spoken by Lucifer to God, these words constitute the first instance and origin of evil. Christianity sees the world and its history as a dramatic struggle between the forces of love and the forces of hatred, between "Thy will be done" and *Non serviam.* The theme of *Ulysses* — not my interpretation or slander of it, but Joyce's own expressed theme — is, therefore, the advancement of hatred.

This is the "final" cause of the disease. The reforming of education, which must begin with the study of the classics, will be sterile and meaningless without a return to the animating principle of our civilization.

When Matthew's father, Thomas Arnold, took on the job of reforming Rugby School in England, he set before himself this purpose, as recounted in Stanley's *Life:*

> His great object [was] the hope of making the school a place of really Christian education . . . . It was not an attempt to give more theological instruction or to introduce sacred words into school administration: His design arose out of the very nature of his office: the relation of an instructor to his pupils was to him like all other relations of human life, only in a healthy state when subordinate to their common relation to God. "The Business of a schoolmaster," he used to say, "no less than that of a parish minister, is the care of souls." The idea of a Christian school, again, was to him the natural result, so to speak, of the very idea of a school in itself . . . . The intellectual training was not for a moment underrated . . . but he looked upon the whole as bearing on the advancement of the one end of all instruction and education; the boys were still treated as schoolboys, but as schoolboys who must grow up to be Christian men . . . . His educa-

tion in short was not . . . based upon religion, but was itself *religious*.

In such a school and with a private and public life shaped by its influence, most of what we object to in our literature and culture in general would atrophy. Putting his ideal negatively, Dr. Arnold said, "What I want to see in the school . . . is an abhorrence of evil." Put positively this means the restoration of its meaning to the word "good."

Thackeray has an essay on "Charity and Humor" that points the way. He is speaking of "humor," but since the principle applies to all literature, let me substitute that word for his:

> "Literature" is wit and love; I am sure, at any rate that the best . . . is that which contains most humanity, that which is flavoured throughout with tenderness and kindness. This love does not demand constant utterance or actual expression, as a good father in conversation with his children or wife is not perpetually embracing them or making protestations of his love; as a lover in the society of his mistress is not, at least as far as I am led to believe, forever squeezing her hand or sighing in her ear, "My soul's darling, I adore you!" He shows his love by his conduct, by his fidelity, by his watchful desire to make the beloved happy; it lightens his eyes when she appears, though he may not speak it; it fills his heart when she is present or absent; influences all his words and actions; suffuses his whole being; it sets the father cheerfully to work through the long day, supports him through the tedious labour of the weary absence or journey, and sends him happy home again, yearning towards the wife and children. This kind of love is not a spasm, but a life. And so with a loving literature; it is the kind, genial spirit's way of looking out on the world.

That is what I mean by the theme of things! Putting his ideal negatively, Dr. Arnold said, "What I want to see in the school . . . is an abhorrence of evil." Put positively that is to say with Thackeray, "the genial spirit's way of looking out on the world."

84

6 Be Ye Therefore Perfect[11]

Freshman college students across the country commonly are assigned some substantial English essay for the latest assault on the old enemy "How to Read." Before us is the title, *Culture and Anarchy: An Essay in Political and Social Criticism.* And then, all alone, on the second page, positively indecent in its nudity, and in italic type, *Estote ergo vos perfecti.* Now what are we going to do with that? Most simply skipped it and went on to the text, catching up with the meaning like an out-of-step soldier on parade, from whatever other words and phrases seemed kindly or familiar — which in Matthew Arnold was not very much. On page two, for example, he says in explanation of a book of maxims, that they are "like a work of doubtless far deeper emotion and power, the *Meditations* of Marcus Aurelius," and further, to make his point even clearer, "that they should be read as Joubert and Nicole should be . . ." and further — still on page two — that "M. Michelet makes it a reproach to us that, in all doubt as to the real author of the *Imitation,* no one has ever dreamed of ascribing that work to an Englishman."

Right at the start of a fair sample of ordinary English prose is a set of obstacles most students simply cannot get over. Vocabulary is one thing, complicated sentence structure still pretty much the same thing. These the diligent student can face with a dictionary and a workbook. But what is he to do with *Estote ergo vos perfecti* and Marcus Aurelius and a book he never heard of, assumed to be so familiar that its short title is given as simply "the *Imitation*" — the imitation of

---

[11]A significant part of this chapter appeared in *Reflections on High School English*, ed. by Gary Tate, Tulsa, Okla., 1966.

85

what? — and who is M. Michelet, let alone Joubert and Nicole?

Communication means a sharing of the wealth; it is the Latin for "common wealth." Words may very well be printed like dollar bills, but we assume real gold in the treasury. Without that commonwealth, we must send our messages by telegram. Without this we can only talk in slogans — which is what we do most of the time. We use language to make animal wants known on the same method of pugnacious repetition by which animals were trained in the experiments of the notorious Pavlov. The mind is not engaged at all. But Arnold — and I take his as a fair sample of normal English prose, not as extraordinarily difficult — begins an essay in political and social criticism, written for the generally educated public, with a Latin phrase from the Vulgate New Testament, spoken by Christ who said, "Be ye therefore perfect," which words, like all good epigraphs, are the refinement, indeed the "perfection" of the thesis. Epigraphs are not little decorations by which an author shows off his learning; in a serious book they are indications of the theme, without which the argument is unintelligible. I was astonished and amused to find this footnote in a great work of contemporary scholarship:

> Even in Matthew Arnold's definition of culture as "the best that has been thought and said in all ages," the original . . . sense of the word as the ideal of man's perfection is obscured. It tends to make culture into a kind of museum.

Professor Jaeger had skipped the epigraph! But with him it was an oversight; with the vast majority of readers it is impossible to do otherwise.

English teachers are unfairly blamed for failing to bear the burden of the entire culture of the West in a few hours per week — everything from the Greeks till now. They get to the point of exasperation at ignorant people who, themselves not knowing how to read, or write like Arnold, say, berate the teacher for Johnny's most popular inability. Of course he cannot read or write — because the commonwealth is spent. The bills are printed with the old faces, but there is no real gold in the king's treasury.

Here is John Ruskin explaining the difference between Gothic and Classical art: another fair sample, a perfectly normal paragraph, not

86

meant to call attention to itself and its author's erudition, but to make the point in the clearest way:

> You may most strictly take the Homeric words describing the aspect of Achilles showing himself on the Greek rampart as representative of the total Greek ideal. Learn by heart unforgettably, the seven lines —

And there follow seven lines of hieroglyphics, unintelligible to students for whom it might be Hebrew, Sanskrit, or perhaps even mathematics — to their teachers it is Greek. But skip it we cannot. Everything that follows is dependent on the meaning. Ruskin says, "representative of the total Greek ideal." This is the heart of his whole chapter on Classical art.

Now what are we going to do? The next time my colleague the chemist says his students cannot read and write, I shall say, "You teach him Latin and Greek, the Bible, classical history, something of the medieval world and the history of modern Europe through World War II — and then I'll teach him to read and write!" And meanwhile stop loading high school and college curricula with dazzling pyrotechnical displays in science and laying down impossible requirements and assignments in science — there are only so many hours in the day! And cool the public propaganda for the experimental sciences, which has created the vicious impression that poetry is for sissies, and stop promoting the poetry of sissies, which is one of the sad side effects. Chemists suffer from the false view that our subject is really like mathematics, a closed system of abstract signs, and therefore will admit of electronic computation and the set method. They think we are lazy, stupid, and perhaps conspiratorial because we have not come up with a device for making wood suddenly into violins — which can be done, but not by programmed texts or among the deaf.

Meanwhile words, phrases, whole passages are skipped, necessarily, and their meaning guessed at, as in the game of hang the butcher, until young people are convinced that literature is an unintelligible joke and that the meaning is really made up by clever readers. As aids to hang the butcher we have assigned specially prepared texts. At the foot of every page, "easy-to-read" explanations of hard words. The text is, as we say, highly glossed, and is exactly the kind we used to have in second-year foreign-language courses. In fact, we have almost got to the point of reading English in translation. At the bottom of page two of Matthew Arnold's text, we find: "Nicole (1625–95) Port-Royalist." But what is a "Port-Royalist"? How could you seriously begin to find that out?

We read English in translation because we have lost all reference to anything. Not only *outside* the words we use by reference to history or other literatures, but even *inside* the words themselves; for words are rich, composite creatures, having meanings and references to meanings within them. Spring this phrase from Belloc on a student: speaking of a movement in English history, he says it was "gradual but rapid." What will they make of that? Or ask them why the phrase "it was manifestly evident" is not so much redundant as ridiculous.

We are suffering from a general depletion of the commonwealth of culture. To change the figure: it took the dust bowl to shake wheat farmers into action in the 1930s. What will it take to shake farmers of men now? If the soil is depleted, what harrow will improve it? Weeds have grown; they have been sown among the wheat. "Some enemy hath done this." There is an enemy between us and the real object of education: Professor Ideology. A new reading method, or the revival of an old one, is not really going to solve anything — Look Jane, See Spot, or old McGuffey either. The crisis in education is not the result of a defect in teaching methods alone, granted that some are better than others and that arguments about them are serious, necessary, and productive. The crisis in education is really the result of a general cultural depletion, and nothing short of a genuine restoration will work any real improvement. And that is no matter for methodology; it is a deeply philosophical, historical, religious, and personal matter, going down into the roots of our civilization and ourselves.

Weakened as we are, I should say to teachers and parents, Look out! The enemy is at the gates, you are about to be invaded or at any rate suffer a series of raids, a vandalism, from the barbaric hordes, pushed down into the colleges from research institutes and the federal government; and from colleges into secondary schools — on all the way to day care centers, the nursery, and, if possible, the womb. I mean simply the attitude toward life that Matthew Arnold called "Philistine" — I have just called it "barbaric," which is against culture and for nothing but what it calls practical and scientific. Its only concern is with getting on in the world. That attitude has put a frightening pressure on education: we are being pressured into false economies, into larger classes, fewer teachers, programmed texts, squads of graduate assistants in basic college courses, and practice teachers and lay assistants in the schools, TV, and teaching machines — all these suggested in the name of "catching up with the twentieth century" or with the Russians. People who tell us to catch up with these two are either evil or ignorant of what the twentieth century really is or the Russians are up to. The function of education is to conserve the cultural organism, to make civilized behavior available to the next generation. What most people mean by the "twentieth century" is barbarism, and by "the Russians" something worse.

"Structuring downward" is in general a bad practice, violating as it does the principle by which all higher forms must respect the integrity and free operation of the lower. Thus, for example, the physician may direct the end of the pharmacist's work but not interfere with it, or parents may direct their children, but not reduce them to instruments. In education this means that high schools have their own job to do and must not be displaced by an invasion from above, that is, from the college; and in turn the college must not become a trial graduate school. Years ago the elementary grades were invaded from above by having bright children "skip," as they called it — thus the "whiz kid," the maladjusted genius.

Education is a relation of student and subject. It must be ordered to the complex and slippery exigencies of both. From the point of view of the student, we should teach what is easiest first; but from the point of view of the subject, this is often impossible. For example, it is commonly acknowledged that logic is a difficult subject. Yet, since it is prerequisite to all other courses in philosophy, willy-nilly it comes first in the sequence and cannot be "skipped." Nor can we propose a radical change in curriculum without carefully considering the development of the student himself as a person. We too often consider him as an abstraction, as a mass in relation to whatever forces might accelerate him.

There are virtues appropriate to childhood. Girls and boys are not little women and little men; and there are subjects and subject matters appropriate to childhood, others appropriate to youth and to maturity. It is more difficult for an adult to learn the names and dates of history, the continents and capitals in geography, or Latin paradigms, than for a child. If a child skips his geography, in order to discuss the political and military problems in Asia, he may never learn where Asia is; and he will suffer a consequent disorder, a disorientation, increasingly common, that forever warps his later political views. The English professor is painfully aware of the "advanced" poetic genius who never learned grammar, as professors of art must be of cubists and abstract impressionists who never learned to draw. Conversely, since politics presupposes ethics, and since ethics cannot be grasped without experience in the world, what are the children to say of Vietnam or Tashkent in the first place? Any pushing up of even the brightest of the immature results in a smart aleck who often dazzles by a display of memorized resemblances — using the virtue proper to the immature, he does well at giving back what he had read and heard. A twelve-year-old might well deserve an "A" in a college course even in so mature a matter as politics because he is able to repeat formulas. He will pass the test, but this is no sign at all of his having grasped the material, or, what is more important, of the discipline having grasped him.

English professors are familiar also with the child who has jumped from *Snow White* to *Lolita* without the intermediate stages: no Rover Boys, no Scott, Mark Twain, or Dickens. A reading list devised at a midwest university recommends what is essentially a college syllabus for high school students — works by Melville, Jane Austen, Thomas Hardy, even Machiavelli, and includes very difficult symbolist stories; Thomas Mann's *Mario and the Magician*, for example, which has as its subject repulsive physical and moral sickness — this for tenth-grade children; and, what is really incomprehensible, a play for the presumably more jaded appetites of the twelfth graders by the Restoration lecher George Wycherly, which is to think of children as nasty little *old* men. You do not advance a child intellectually or morally by force-feeding him mature and, in these cases, decadent "adult" fare. You do not improve or advance a high school curriculum by running trial heats of college courses over it. High school teachers filch the college reading lists in the hope of preparing their students for college courses when the right preparation is to cover prerequisite material. In an age so concerned with civil rights, we should not overlook the rights of childhood.

It is true that there are high school courses taught in college that should be moved back. But the meaning of "advanced placement" must not be stretched to cover what is really a problem in curriculum. We have grades — steps — necessary to the development of the student and to the structure of the subject. If you want to study philosophy, you must begin with logic; and if you want to make a young man into a philosopher, you must get him into the habit of being logical by drill in its disciplines. Some will go faster than others and that is why we have that other kind of "grade" from "A" to "F". But logic cannot be skipped nor can any test be substituted for it. Again, a smart boy can bone up on the rules of logic, but he will not have assimilated the terms or acquired the permanent disposition. A Chinese once criticized American education by saying, "You are always pulling on the flower to make it grow faster." We need rather, in the words of T. S. Eliot, a "life of significant soil." If a student has a greater capacity to learn, all the more reason for him to complete the full four years of his high school life and the full four years of his college life so that he actually realizes his potential. Slow him down. At Princeton, under Dean Root, the students in the four-year college normally took five courses per year; the exceptionally bright ones were permitted to take four, on the grounds that for them it was really worthwhile to go slow. An education is not an annoying impediment to research or business, but a good in itself, indispensable to the development of the qualified person.

There is a well-known distinction, often cited and seldom really seen, between the horizontal extension of knowledge and the vertical ascent to higher planes. For example, it is obvious that a knowledge of carpentry can be extended horizontally in the practice of the craft — a man can learn more and more simply by doing a certain thing again and again, like laying a floor; and his knowledge can also be extended by the application of this skill to different things — from floors to staircases, windows, roofs. He will have learned by practice and application more and more about the same operations.

But consider the knowledge of the architect, which includes carpentry — not the practice of carpentry, but its reasons. The architect, in considering the principles of building as a whole, must know the reason why. Not how, but why. All the knowledge of all carpenters, indefinitely extended, will never add up to that of the least of architects, and the least of architects, though he has not the skill to do it, understands the reasons for the best of carpentry beyond the carpenter himself. The architect, from a higher prospect, sees the reasons for what carpenters, masons, tilers, glaziers do. He sees the reasons for those things and integrates them. He does not simply coordinate, that is, order disparate lines of activity the way a foreman does; he *integrates* them, he sees them as parts of an *integer* or whole. Floor, staircase, window, roof are not coordinates, but parts that together make up the house. They are constitutive elements of the thing, the one, whole, integral thing. But suppose all knowledge is an integer!

There is a famous picture coming down to us in different versions from the Middle Ages, illustrating education. It depicts a several-storied tower into which the schoolboy with his satchel and his tablet enters on the ground floor, greeted by the stern *magister*, who has merry eyes, a big stick called a *baculum*, and a book called the *Donatus* from its author, the fourth-century grammarian. Next, through the window of the second story, we see the boy progress to Aristotle's *Logic*, and at the third window up to Cicero's *Rhetoric*.

Rhetoric is the liberal art of intellectual nourishment, as cooking is the servile art of physical nourishment. Rhetoric makes the truth effective. It is not simply more and more grammar or more and more logic, any more than cooking is more and more vegetables. Rhetoric is rather making something out of the sentences and the arguments that grammar and logic have supplied. Rhetoric is grammar and logic. Any piece of rhetoric is made up of grammar and logic; they are its constitutive parts. From the point of view of the higher prospect of rhetoric, one looks down on grammar and logic and sees the reasons for their operations.

These liberal arts differ from one another vertically. You rise from one to the other, not by a horizontal extension, but a vertical ascent to a different level of understanding that includes the lower ones, analogous to the relation of part to whole.

In the picture, the boy, grown up to adolescence, climbs from the fourth to the seventh window, entering the higher stories of arithmetic, geometry, music, and astronomy; beyond which the young man climbs higher still, up to philosophy, comprising physics, biology, psychology, ethics, economics, politics; to metaphysics and the highest peak, theology, the study of the mind of God who knows and made all things — in Whom, therefore, the universe and all knowledge is integral.

The brave young man at the top of the stairs must now descend to wherever in the scale of work his talents lie, learning how to do one thing in the daily practice of an art or craft, but having had a vision of its place in the universal scheme of things in which architects cannot be arrogant or carpenters envious, because they both are parts of something greater than themselves. That is the difference between a technical school and a university — the university is supposed to rise to the universal. It integrates the horizontal in the vertical. It is a place where "young men see visions and old men dream dreams."

Teaching, Plato says, is a species of friendship, whose highest degree is love, in which persons see each other as integral parts of something greater than themselves — a marriage, a family, a college, a nation, a faith. In the pursuit of happiness, in marriage or friendship, in vocations, recreation, politics, and just plain jobs — in the long run — we have to ask what the whole thing is: What are all those activities and commitments parts of? *What is the integer?* If a student forgets everything he learned at school or college, he had best remember this one question. It will be on the very final examination that his own conscience will make at the last hour of his life: In the pursuit of horizons — of horizontal things — have you failed to raise your eyes and mind and heart up to the stars, to the reason for things, and beyond, as Dante says at the top of the tower of his poem:

> To the love which moves the sun
> And all the other stars?

Of course we are all in favor of advanced placement in the ordinary sense. If a freshman at college already had two years of high school Latin, he should not begin again with *amo, amas, amat*. He should be placed in the third year course. If that is what is meant, we should all be for it. If a student has had plane geometry in high school, let him go on to solid in college. It is difficult to adjust these matters. There are differences from school to school, and overlaps from school to college; so the placement test is called upon. Certainly a student should not be forced to take the same course twice, nor should he be given college credit for a course for which he got high school credit — this would be to receive payment twice for the same work done. But once the placement test comes into use there is a strong temptation for the teacher in the senior year of high school to give up the subject in favor of a year's intense drill in how to get high scores. Even worse, some universities — and famous ones — are granting college credit to students passing these tests without the genuine experience of a course. This is like trafficking in indulgences; it is a selling of credit in the absence of merit and is a kind of fraud. A smart boy can run four years of college tests and call himself a Bachelor of Arts, when in fact he will be a neurotic with a talent for running tests. Do we detect an adulteration of learning in the name of economy? Credit without courses — which means without teachers, classrooms, electric lights, and heat?

A test is not the equivalent of a course. What we test is only that aspect of the experience which is testable. In some disciplines that aspect includes greater amounts of the reality than in others; in none does it include the whole; and in many — especially the humanities — it includes very little. If a student cannot respond to the testable aspect of a discipline to which he had submitted for the required length of time, we infer that he has not sufficiently responded to the whole. But this does not work the other way around: If a student bones up on the testable aspects of a subject — not having submitted to the discipline — the grade he gets on a test in no way implies a corresponding response to the whole. He has not had the whole, so how could he respond? That some students are fast and some slow has no logical relation whatsoever to the selling of indulgenced tests.

Structuring downward from the graduate school to the college has resulted in the sad fact that colleges with fine old names have become marketplaces for a series of tests, with quickie courses in how to pass them taught by graduate assistants whose minds are on their PhDs. Liberal education has all but been eliminated. The high prestige these places still obtain is from their graduate schools and from their past. Advanced placement has ruined the college by advancing the graduate school downward into it; the high school has been ruined by advancing the college downward into it. One can dream nightmares not far from waking life in which nuclear fission is taught in the nursery. It may be done; but there will be thumb-sucking at Los Alamos.

It follows, then, that we should certainly place students in the courses they have had prerequisites to, that we eliminate duplications in high school and college curricula, and that schools, libraries, theaters, publications should work together to enrich the life of significant soil and foster a genuine growth of the intellectual life of every community. Mark Van Doren called college "a vacation from the commonplace. It is a time," he said "when we are not merely expected to change, but required to." It is that change, that growth of the person both in intellect and will, that transformation of his deepest life, which is the untestable — by no means detestable — reality of education. It cannot be speeded up or skipped or rearranged to suit the economy or the race with Russia or the latest machine. Education is a very great good in itself and not a mere instrument of success. The end of education is the perfection of each person and our special care is to prevent the emergence of the irrational aesthete and the brutal scientist. In the most serious, not the merely snobbish, sense of the word, we should have in mind the cultivation of "gentlemen."

And teachers must start with themselves. It is the same with teaching as with any calling, good or bad — it is a person who does it. No one ever learned from a method any more than he was ever killed by a gun or a knife. We learn and are killed by persons who may or may not use various instruments. The first rule for a teacher, then, as for any person, is to be somebody worthy of his calling, having an appropriate "dignity," whose Latin root means "worthiness," which by no means implies that he should act like an undertaker. There is a dignity appropriate to taking us under and another to taking young people up. I mean the right worth for the job, and for the teacher of English or the classics this means a high seriousness about language and literature in the presence of which slovenliness and disrespect do not occur, simply as a matter of courtesy. This cliche happens to be true: if you want to teach something, you must have that something yourself. If poetry is not a part of your life, no method in the classroom will create *ex nihilo* the love of poetry in your students. Recall the famous dictum of St. Augustine: Love God and do what you will. It is open to a grave misuse, but the essential truth of it stands. The same maxim applies to what we call "English": Love literature and do what you will.

Why are students coming down from high schools and colleges — even after four years and a bachelor's degree — so appallingly deficient they cannot read a normal paragraph in Matthew Arnold, a popular writer of less than one hundred years ago? It is because, as Ezra Pound said, "they ain't got no kulchur." If there were music, poetry, and art at home, they would have learned despite bad teaching — teaching has always been mostly bad. Do you suppose Shelley's schoolmasters were much good, laying about with the cane? Yet he wrote very well at the age of eighteen. Our boys have simply not had the nourishment. Their cultural life has been exhausted. Teachers have sown the seeds of poetry and prose according to the directions on the package, and have tried different varieties of seed; but the soil is gone. To see these shriveled persons coming up to college year after year now is to ask who in their lives has loved literature. Where could they have found the spiritual environment absolutely essential to the germination of the seed? I am not speaking of sentimental gush about books by someone who himself watches TV or at best reads the latest novels. This is the danger in St. Augustine's phrase. Love presupposes knowledge. Love without knowledge is sentimentality, an indirect form of hatred that adds deception to contempt, so that one actively loves what is not really there — something worse than no love at all. Remember the word dignity — a worthiness. A person who is to be worthy of his job must have a love that is genuine.

The first quiet but definite step in the genuine reformation of education is that parents and teachers should read. Beginning with themselves, wherever they are and in whatever stage in their own depletion — they must read. Not the one hundred greatest books, or any of those they think they *ought* to read, but whatever good book is at hand; and beginning with it, come not just to like it, but to know it and to love it — and then rightly read another and another. I vividly remember standing before a fine teacher at college who had done a lot to promote the hundred great books and saying to him, "But I just can't read all those books!" In the middle of the *Critique of Pure Reason* I had despaired. "Of course you can't," Mark Van Doren said. "Nobody can read a hundred books; but here is one — read that." He took a volume from his desk haphazardly and handed it to me — it happened to be a collection of Plato's *Dialogues* that helped to change my life. Of course, I never finished them; I am still reading Plato because I have not yet finished my life.

Ideology is the enemy. He has a nasty brother named Enthusiasm. The enthusiastic teacher is the one who rushes into a subject fervently but in ignorance on the grounds that action is virtue and that keeping the class awake for fifty minutes is the real business at hand. The enthusiast not only makes a fool of himself in front of those narrow-

96

eyed and shrewd youths who see right through him, but worse, he often makes fools of those less shrewd, open-eyed, and best — because trusting — students whom he really teaches, but teaches to be shallow. He turns out those smart literary types who talk about Kant, Kafka, and the *Tropic of Capricorn* but have never experienced the copulative relation between a subject and a predicate. John Ruskin wrote:

> Do not talk but of what you know; do not think but of what you have materials to think justly upon; and do not look for things only that you like, when there are others to be seen: This is the lesson to be taught to our youth, and inbred in them: and that mainly by our own example and contriteness. Never teach a child anything of which you are not sure yourself; and, above all, if you feel anxious to force anything into its mind in tender years, that the virtue of youth and early association may fasten it there, be sure it is no lie which you thus sanctify. There is always more to be taught of absolute, incontrovertible knowledge, open to its capacity, than any child can learn; there is no need to teach it anything doubtful. Better that it should be ignorant of a thousand truths, than have consecrated in its heart a single lie.

Stick to a few incontrovertibly good books and to a few real principles of grammar and rhetoric, and stay away from itchy reading lists and above all stay away from those interminably arid — stupid — discussions of current events that have almost displaced the serious study of history and literature. It is appalling to see little boys and girls on television shows aged in current events like so many intellectual dwarfs, little but old and pinched in the face, smoking as it were Cuban cigars of current events, midgets at a circus of politics discussing what should be done in Africa but prematurely denied the childhood knowledge of the Great Gray-Green Greasy Limpopo River; discussing foreign policy on Cuba when they do not know the formal beauty in the statement that Cuba is an island bounded by the Atlantic Ocean, the Straits of Florida, and the Caribbean Sea. *There* is an incontrovertible truth, while the rest is material they have no grounds "for thinking justly on," whatever their opinions might be;

and the result of an education of that kind is the youth who has opinions about everything and the truth of nothing, even to the point of coming to that sorry disposition of the mind so common at college in which truth is denied altogether. "What is truth?" they say, failing to note that Pontius Pilate asked the same question before sending an innocent Man to the cross.

> The letter of the *Times* correspondent referred to contained an account of one of the most singular cases of depravity ever brought before a criminal court; but it is unnecessary to bring any of its details under the reader's attention, for nearly every other number of our journals has of late contained some instances of atrocities before unthought of, and, it might have seemed, impossible to humanity. The connection of these with the modern love of excitement in the sensation novel and drama may not be generally understood, but it is direct and constant; all furious pursuit of pleasure ending in actual desire of horror and delight in death.

That is, again, from Ruskin, written almost one hundred years ago and relevant right now: schools have direct responsibility in this shocking fact — or perhaps it is no longer shocking, and that is far worse — that a child or woman cannot safely walk the streets of any city in the United States after ten o'clock at night, not even the streets of mine, a university town, isolated, without the usual sociological excuses. Anyone even slightly acquainted with history knows that we should be alarmed, not only for our wives and children, but alarmed at the ultimate barbarism of which this is an early, unmistakable symptom. We should add to Ruskin's paragraph, the increased power in methodology that has broadened the sensation novel to include the movie and the television show.

We must work very hard to restore first in ourselves and then, by influence in others, opposed to that "furious pursuit of pleasure ending in actual desire of horror and delight in death," the pursuit of truth, ending in actual desire of beauty and delight in life.

7 To Each His Own[12]

Freedom, in the popular imagination, means doing what you want. A man has the right to do anything he wants, provided it does not hurt anyone else or interfere with anyone else. That is the popular view and, although there are definitions more sophisticated, subtler, and more precise, philosophers have agreed that in establishing the general meaning of words we should follow the usage of the people, making things more explicit in the light of philosophical principle. Justice in the popular imagination is that minimum amount of coercion necessary to permit freedom.

Almost everyone agrees that we have not reached a state of perfect justice. Nobody can do exactly what he wants. In fact there are some people who want to tear up the laws because they have not got justice, that is, because they have not got what they want.

Now if we believe in justice, and if justice gives us freedom, and if freedom is doing what everybody wants — how are we going to get it when what some people want directly violates what other people want? When you think about it abstractly, the problem is insoluble. But concretely, among any real group of people, if freedom means doing what you want, a free society can exist anytime men are agreed on what they want. A society may be called just when a determinate number agree. There will always be a minority of dissidents who for one reason or another will not fit, but the determinate number set the tone of a society; and all its laws, all the rules and regulations of that society, the traffic laws, the criminal laws, the tax and banking laws,

<hr>

[12] A substantial part of this chapter appeared in the *Journal of the Kansas Bar Association*, 39 (Winter 1970).

all the instruments of justice, are based on this cultural fact — that the vast majority want to do the same things. They are in cultural agreement, they share a spirit, a common ground.

If ninety-five percent of Americans did what they wanted today, things would not be substantially different from the way they have been at least these hundred years of the Republic since the Civil War. People have always pretty much done what they really wanted. Most of us want to stop at traffic lights, most of us want to drive reasonably safely at least most of the time, most of us want to live peacefully with one another, we want to speak to one another honestly and decently and to enjoy each others' confidence and commerce. Most of us even want to pay our taxes and fight our wars. Some may not, and the rest may complain, and everybody slips now and then — but the job gets done. America is part of Western civilization, of European — what is most properly called Christian — culture; and the European philosophical tradition teaches that this common usage of the people is actually a reflection of immutable Natural Law, which, Christianity says, is ultimately rooted in the will of God.

This does not mean that everyone, or even the majority, actually follows philosophical teaching or practices Christianity, but that a determinate number do. Nor does it mean that even the determinate number are in explicit agreement on the great philosophical questions or even on what Christianity is. I am not talking about schools of thought or creeds, about definitions and confessions, but about a common sense. The skeptic as much as the believer — G.B. Shaw as much as G.K. Chesterton — agrees about the basic things. When the Founding Fathers wrote about "life, liberty, and the pursuit of happiness," they had the Christian sense of those words in mind. They wrote in the context of eighteen hundred years of Christian culture — the common sense, the *sensus populorum*, on which any political order must be based. People differ in creed; some are even atheists. People differ in politics; some are even anarchists. They differ about art, music, manners, morals. We always have and always will, but there has been a common sense, unquestioned, beyond which there was only the unimaginable, the unspeakable, the abomination that had no name and, if touched inadvertently in some particular act, it gave all sides in any dispute a sense of horror and disgust.

The Donner Party, for example, in the Gold Rush days, stranded in the High Sierras, and recently a soccer team, crashed in the

100

Cordilleras, committed cannibalism: the survivors ate the dead bodies of their friends, an act outside the common sense. Now when we say freedom is doing what you want, we assume that no one wants to be a cannibal. Suppose one does, what then? Voltaire said in the famous phrase: "I disagree with what you say but will defend to the death your right to say it." That is admirable. That is right. We all agree to that. But, of course, the key word is "you" — I disagree with "you." I disagree with a normal human being, not a beast. Voltaire did not mean that he would defend to the death a man's right to eat his neighbor. Thoreau taught civil disobedience. He was a civil man. You might agree or disagree with his position on slavery or taxes, but there is no question that by civil disobedience he meant behavior well within the bounds of Christian culture. He was horrified to discover what kind of a fanatic John Brown really was. Even when it came to war, Generals Lee and Grant were willing to fight to the death for a political and social cause, but nonetheless, even to the death, they operated within the bounds of culture; they were Christian gentlemen, honorable in victory and defeat. We have fought wars according to the rules. Even in our hatreds, in our anger, in our rage at one another, we are only free to fight about what we both ultimately want.

The problem in America today is that we have met the cannibal, the assassin, the pervert, the abomination, and we simply do not know what to do with him. We are committed to justice, to the proposition that everyone has the right to do what he wants, and we have met people who want to do — not just things we disagree with, like Voltaire — but things that cannot be done. And yet these people do them.

At universities across the country a few years ago, a subcultural creature used to blow his nose publicly on the American flag. Authoritative University Opinion said: Suspend judgment until it can be ascertained that it was an official flag of the United States; perhaps it might be found to have an unofficial fiber content. Call it anything, so long as you do not face the fact of what was done — not simply an illegal act, but a disgrace — because Authority does not know how to handle a disgrace. The student union building is gutted by an arsonist. The work of some poor fellow suffering from mental illness, we are told by Authoritative Opinion. A solitary pyromaniac. When fires break out all over town, it is admitted that there may be several solitary pyromaniacs. When firemen are shot at by snipers, it is presumed that there are several types of solitary mental illness — that solitary mental illness is ubiquitous. Is there one illness in a dozen persons or one person with a dozen illnesses? Anything but face the fact of what is happening. Obscene, abhorrent words are scrawled on walls and sidewalks. In front of the library a pervert sells lewd magazines. We witnessed in those years a moral fungus growing, day after day, with an increasing virulence beneath the norms of culture — an alien thing. It was not a matter of law and order and justice. What we faced was not any recognized criminal threat, nor was it political, religious, or philosophical dissent. It was the presence of an alien thing.

Here is a quotation from a book about freedom and justice, about doing what you want, called *Do It!*

> Every high school and college in the country will close with riots and sabotage and cops will circle the campuses, standing shoulder to shoulder. The schools belong to the pigs. Millions of young people will surge into the streets of every city, dancing, singing, smoking pot, f ------ in the streets.

There has been stuff like this circulating in the subway urinals; there has been stuff like this in cheap hotels — and expensive ones, I suppose — we all know that. There has always been stuff like this in the medical journals. But in my town, a quiet city in the heart of America, with the usual jobs done well and badly, with justice and injustice rather imperfectly distributed, but, take the world all in all, a good town, proud of its freedom and its university — in this town, every single word of that repulsive prophecy happened, including the participation of schoolchildren.

One or two percent of any society is always subcultural. The Trotskyite, the Communist, the arsonist, the homosexual, the assassin — these are obviously dangerous and the courts must dispose their cases. Law has its problems. I shall not underestimate them; but law is not *the* problem. The enemy I am talking about is the one lurking in the guts of the whole nation like an invisible and deadly virus. It is not an action, but an attitude that says everyone has the right to arson, murder, rape, because doing those things is necessarily included under the rubric of freedom, of doing what one wants — not what I want or you want, but what someone wants. In a word, we have raised the abnormal and aberrant to the condition of a human right. The beast is loose among us, and he is welcome in our universities and homes. An alien thing is tearing at the vitals of all order, all law, all justice; and we must — but we will not — expel it. Let it grow and we shall have a bloodbath. Whenever in history this has happened, in Rome with Catiline, in the Middle Ages with the Albigensians, in Germany with National Socialism, whenever that abomination has seized power, the only response has been extermination — it or us.

It came to this in the United States in 1970. My home town was under martial law. The National Guard patrolled the streets. The schools were closed just as they said. They strung piano wire at neck-height in alleys, threw fire bombs and fled, hoping to catch the "pigs," as they called them, by their naked throats. It came to this. It was studiously overlooked and we forget, rebuild, patch up, grant amnesty and overlook again — because the thing is still here and will awake any time it wants. It dreams and feeds on popcorn in the movies, purrs on hi-fi sets, "swinges its scaly tail" contentedly in magazines. I am not talking about legal definitions of pornography and treason. This is beneath the courts. It is the sort of thing a leader of the Students for a Democratic Society reported, speaking of the Sharon Tate murders:

> First they killed those pigs, then they ate dinner in the
> same room with them, then they even shoved a fork into
> the victim's stomach. Wild!

Or from an obituary in the once irreverent but decent *New Yorker* magazine of a Pulitzer Prize-winning poetess — this is the smiling face that grins in middle-class living rooms, in dentists' offices. The *New Yorker*, lamenting this famous lady's loss, prints in tribute a poem of hers as her own epitaph, which says:

> Come, drunks and drug-takers;
>   come, perverts unnerved,
> Receive the laurel . . .
> Parochial punks, trimmers, nice
>   people, joiners true blue,
> Get the hell out of the way.

The laurel is the crown of poetry and poetry the principal medium of cultural life. America is not sick. The *New Yorker* is sick. The American people have not lost their common sense of decency and shame, but the enemy is at the switchboards and people are confused, reactions are paralyzed. The two percent is loose. The pervert wears the laurel; the arsonist and the rioter, the crown. You will find this scum collected in pools and drains all over our cultural life — and we must get rid of it. Get the movies out of town. Get the books out of the local drugstores where the children go, and out of the schools, for God's sake! Not by going to court or the Parent-Teachers' meetings. The courts cannot punish a cultural disease. Tell the druggist that stuff is intolerable. Take your business elsewhere. Expel the handful of faculty and students in the schools and universities who have been corrupted by this thing. You can find out who they are — it is not hard. The children know. Punishment can only do them good; it is the only way to help them. They need the rule. It is the rule that comforts them. They know it themselves; they need to be kept from going too far, from falling apart altogether. I wonder, if a cannibal had come to college and eaten his breakfast of human flesh at the cafeteria, whether our Joint Student-Faculty Committee on Discipline and our chancellor and deans would not in an embarrassed way have sat down at his table — not to eat of course, but perhaps at least . . . the positive approach: a scholarship, an appointment to the faculty to teach a course in it, a new program with federal support, a laboratory with different size pots! Expulsion? Perish the thought. Then perish the university.

If you get rid of all that now, you will not have the rifles and the fire bombs; and if you do not, they will be back and you will have burnt buildings and burnt people. The normal instruments for the restoration of culture must be used. For universities they are these:

First, negative and immediate. Expulsion. A university is not Hyde Park; it is not Haight Ashbury or Greenwich Village. It is not a brothel or a cabaret. A decorum, a decency, high seriousness, a zeal for truth and beauty — the word *student* means "zealous" in Latin — these are the necessary modes of behavior at a university. Declare a moratorium on microphones. Ban the bullhorns. Stop the teach-ins, the mass hysteria, the politicalization, the emotionalization, the almost total irrationalization of the campus, and get back to classrooms and laboratories, and subjects. Study, learn the tough and only way to learn from a teacher: with a subject and some discipline. A student or a member of the faculty is a representative of the norms of culture without which society cannot exist; a university is precisely the place where the two percent of cultural dissidents — not political or intellectual dissidents — the two percent who really do not believe in freedom, who do not believe in civilization but opt for savagery, cannot be tolerated.

And the second instrument of repossession, the positive: You must find the right kind of teacher. Universities across the nation have put a premium on research and let the teaching slide. Classroom teaching has sunk to an appalling mess. It is no wonder students listen to the Maharishi or the latest moral arsonist. A university is not a research institute; it is essentially for the transmission of culture, the transmission of the thing on which all else, including research, is based. If you get someone into science, philosophy, or literature, if you get him into Plato or Newton or Shakespeare, he will see for himself why men have fought and died for civilization. Get a young man into science or philosophy, and he is not going to fool around with student or any other kind of radical politics. So teaching is first. And the first quality of the teacher is his own freedom, his moral rectitude, his character. We want a good man — strong, temperate, prudent, just. Second, he must have a knack for teaching his subject. He must have a certain fire, a certain spirit, a certain personality. There are many different kinds, a thousand kinds — some fast, some slow, some obvious, public and spectacular, good for lectures; others more private, personal, excellent in seminars and conference. But in every case a competence in the communication of the subject must be there.

And the subject is not a specialized knowledge or technique. The subject is not chemistry, though a teacher may use chemistry as the particular means by which he gets the student to know what science is, because science, the systematic search for truth, is one of the tap roots of culture. The subject is not poetic structure, though a teacher may use a poem as the particular means by which he gets the student to know what literature is, what art is — because these are roots also. And third, if in addition a teacher does research and publishes, there is nothing wrong with that: it is not to be ignored, but put third. First we want a man, second we want a gentleman, and third we want a technician.

I have spoken of universities because I know them. The same

105

principles apply to every walk of life — business, government; every institution, secular and religious. When you choose a writer, a clergyman, a newsman, an actor, a banker, an insurance man, a lawyer, a shopkeeper, a druggist, a doctor, a used-car salesman, an undertaker — anybody at all who has to do a job — you want first a man, a good man. And next he must communicate, know how to share more than his skill. He has got to share himself on the common level of mankind. He has got to have a common culture; not a fancy thing, not "la-de-da," but the common sense, the plain, ordinary way of the American people. Third, he must be technically excellent; he must know the bookkeeping, the tensile strengths, how to wire the gadget, how to nail down the coffin lid. We have been too high on technique and have often put it in the service of bad taste, and worse, of bad or indifferent morals — and the right order must be reestablished.

I am saying something very simple and obvious: An alien thing has got into positions of cultural power. It is at the switchboards. And the time has come for the people to repossess them. Universities are not the causes of national distress, but the victims. Do not be fooled by student and faculty spokesmen — the real majority do not participate in college politics; they are too busy at the full-time business of education and have not got the expert advice of professional agitators — or the money. Many students and members of the faculties strongly urge official intervention in university affairs to ensure the public safety and the quiet pursuit of education free from insult and harassment. In the escalated rhetoric, a false polarity has been created by which the general public is opposed to faculties and students — we hear about the "thinking of the young," "what youth thinks," and "university opinion," whereas the real opposition is between, on the one hand, very small and vicious pressure groups together with their larger number of sympathizers and, on the other, *all the rest of us.*

Universities are particularly vulnerable in this age of technology. Tens of thousands of adolescents, immature, cut off from home, locked up with a high-strung, frequently neurotic, if spasmodically brilliant, faculty of specialists in a billion-dollar sandbox — what do you expect? We need an interchange, a great inrush of ordinary reality, an aeration, a suffusion of sunlight and air. The universities cannot reform themselves. The people must repossess them at the polls, by vote and through the normal political procedures — letters to governors, senators, boards of trustees. You have more than the right; you have the obligation to see to it that your children get the kind of education you want. If you are liberal, if you really believe in Voltaire, John Stuart Mill, the Bill of Rights, the Rights of Man — if you believe that justice is freedom and freedom to let men do what they want — it is absolutely necessary to see that these freedoms can only be maintained by members of the human race. The rights of man means at least the rights of *man*, not anything less.

Who is to say? Who is to say what is human and what is not? You are, I am. We, the people, bewildered, unbelieving, utterly amazed and paralyzed at his hitherto unimaginable extrusion. We must come to our common senses and throw it out before someone — everyone — gets really hurt. Witchhunts? Inquisitions? Censorship? Not at all. Every man has the right to speak, to write, to teach the truth as he sees it. That is precisely what we must defend. We are in Germany in 1931, in Russia in 1916. Yeats said: "The best lack all conviction while the worst are full of passionate intensity . . . . And everywhere the ceremony of innocence is drowned." The soldier in the barracks brawl says, "You can call me that, my cousin, my brother, and maybe my father that; but if you call my sister that, or my mother that, I'll bust you in the nose!" Well, they are getting too close to our sisters and our mothers, and if anyone does not see this, it is because he has not got a sister or a mother, or a university, or a city, or a nation, or a God.

A vicious sentimentalism is poisoning the wells. It is in the universities and colleges, the churches, the entertainment industry generally — movies, television, newspapers, magazines, popular songs — in the wells from which we get our spiritual drink, from which our whole cultural life is irrigated.

Let's clean them out with the purification of return to principles. All reasoned demonstration begins with something given — in geometry, for example, that the whole is greater than the part — which itself cannot be proved. A principle in any order is precisely what cannot be proved in that order. The word *principle*, as we know, in Latin means "beginning," "that before which there is nothing." To deny the beginning vitiates the subject. In politics and ethics generally, of which politics is a branch, the given is what in general we call civilization or culture, opposed to which is savagery. Civilization is a complex web of givens from which we demonstrate practical conclusions in law and manners. All the strands of this web go back to some

107

very few original fibers that we call *first* principles, which are not culturally given but self-evident; and the first principle of all in the ethical order is to do the good. If a man denies that, he denies morality itself. First principles are so obvious they are difficult to see — the "self-evident" is not so evident always to us — and especially difficult to formulate and defend. But no one can deny them without making use of them. If you deny the good, you have to prove that it is a "good" thing to deny the good.

Justice is simply the social good, and it must therefore be done. It is defined as "giving each his due" — *cuique suum*, "to each his own." A man is due his life because he is a living thing; it is his nature to have life; and, since it is also his nature to be moral, if a man commits a crime, he must be punished because punishment is retributive — punishment is the penalty due the criminal in justice to him. Proportioned punishment is due him, too, and you cannot deny him that right without yourself committing an injustice against him deserving punishment in turn. The judge who fails the criminal in punishment himself incurs a greater guilt.

Sentimentalism is not just a weakness, and is certainly not a virtue — it is confused with mercy — but a crime; and vicious sentimentalism is ordinary sentimentality raised up in place of principle. It is, as I said, poisoning the wells.

It is not this or that law or this or that case, but law itself, justice itself that has been challenged, and it is only at the level of first principles that a proper defense can be made. The crisis in law and order today is not a legal one. It is a disaster at the level of first principles. Not just the courts but our whole civilization sickens as it spreads.

Sentimentalism, as the constitutive parts of the word imply, is the subjugation of the "mental" to the "sentient." It is an attempt to found a philosophy on feeling. Man has sentiments, of course. It is unreasonable, in the name of reason, to exclude them. Man is a rational animal, and one of the first things his reason tells him is that animals are sentient and therefore that man has feelings. Sentiments, if subject to the reason, give it force, color, alacrity, and verve. Sentiment is good. Sentimentality is "subjecting reason to desire," as Dante says of carnal sinners in the *Inferno*, putting reason to the use of feeling rather than the right way around. Gluttons, for example, spend their intelligence in the service of their bellies; and so it is with the avaricious

108

and those who cannot control their tempers or who are infantile about sex. Mere sentimentality is a pathetic thing. It is the vice of weak people, disdained rather than abhorred, an object of ridicule rather than wrath. Everyone at parties knows the pornographic bore who cannot get his mind above his loins and his contraceptive wife who cannot get his loins below her mind; you hope they grow up and learn about love and sacrifice. In business everybody knows the ruthless dolt who does everything for money, for whom everything is for sale, who subjects recreation, friendship, even his marriage and his family to success and ruins all conversation with perpetual derision of everything except what pays.

But sentimentalism is worse than sentimentality. The merely sentimental man does what he feels like doing without thinking. The doctrine of sentimentalism asserts that thought is an instrument in the service of doing what one feels like. The sentimentalist does not simply subject reason to desire; he denies the difference. He reduces reason to desire and says all problems are essentially emotional or environmental.

Karl Menninger, the dean of psychoanalysts, had another of his best sellers out recently called *The Crime of Punishment*, a kind of psychological soap opera. The title had been used before by a certain Margaret Wilson, who many years ago wrote another sentimental potboiler called *My Six Convicts* — this was back in the 1930s. One knows the sort of thing. You find the attitude in pet magazines: "My Six Pekineses," or in the *National Geographic* with Lady Jane Goodall and her chimpanzees. It is as repugnant to the dignity of dogs to dress them up like people and parade them on tightropes in circuses as it is for people to live with apes. The ancient legend tells how Romulus and Remus were suckled by a she-wolf under a divine movement toward the founding of Rome. Tarzan lived as lord of the jungle, talking with monkeys and wrestling with crocodiles. But anthropologists today nurse infant apes and coddle convicts.

Since a convict is a man, it is wrong to treat him like a pet. He possesses a dignity according to his nature, having intelligence and will; and he has the right to a just punishment proportioned to his crime. No crime is so atrocious as to deserve the visitations of a social worker. A first class embezzler scarcely deserves the indignity of Dr. Menninger's condescending therapy, or a jewel thief whose skill has made him world-renowned, or a kidnapper or rapist for that matter.

Thoreau once said that if he knew someone was coming to his front door with the special, premeditated intention of doing him good, he would escape through the back door at the first knock. A self-respecting convict pursued by a rehabilitator should be guiltless if in self-defense he kicked him down the famous road of his good intentions — or her, because sentimentalism is frequently the vice of silly women in tough professions where they do not belong.

There is another justification for punishment besides retribution. Pain and deprivation are medicinal. They hurt so much that the criminal can learn that crime does not pay — or at least that victims pay back. If you want to teach the prisoner a trade or put him to useful work, well and good; but those things are secondary and must never interfere with the first and proper use of punishment, which is the restoration of the equality of justice not only in society but in the person of the criminal. A person who commits a crime has indulged his will against his reason; a disequilibrium has been established in his soul, as Plato says, which can only be righted by a retributive exercise of reason against his will. The greatest evil in the world is to do wrong without being punished. A prison therefore is not a hospital, not a school, certainly not a hotel or place of entertainment — though it may act secondarily in all those ways. First and properly, a prison is a place of punishment that hurts.

The sentimentalists begin with capital punishment, which they say is always wrong because it leaves no room for self-improvement. But punishment is improvement of the self even when the criminal refuses to admit it. He is at least as much less wicked as he suffers pain — there is a balance of hurt against hurt, eye for eye, tooth for tooth that puts him in the order of justice, even against his will. If crime were merely sickness, the sentimentalists would be right, or if men were merely animals. They say capital punishment is so final; but murder is final. We are not talking about degrees of crime and punishment, which must be balanced, but the nature of the thing. It is not really *capital* punishment that bothers sentimentalists, though they use it as the cutting edge of their argument. They object to punishment itself; and that is because they deny the existence of justice; and that is because they deny that man is free, that man is responsible for his acts. Crime, they say, is sickness. It must be cured or, better, prevented by a prophylaxis of the spirit, by the extermination of free will altogether so that men will react like Pavlov's dogs to sensitivity training and even to psychosurgery and drugs. Crime, they say, is caused by a psychological malfunction. It is unjust, they say, to punish a man for heart disease and so unjust to punish him for theft.

Unjust? Yes, they use the word whose meaning they deny. As C.S. Lewis said, sentimentalists propose a view of the universe from which they "except themselves." They say crime is illness. Now if that were true, there could be no moral act whatsoever. If man is not free to choose evil, he is not free to choose good. An accidental confluence of forces puts one on this or that end of the hangman's rope. If murder is a disease, the victim is killed by this disease called murder through the agency of this innocent carrier, Jack the Ripper, just as pneumonia kills through the agency of an innocent virus. There is nothing "due" anyone or anything. Everything that lives will die. The Lord giveth and the Lord taketh away through natural processes: crime is chemistry. Then so is all behavior. If man is not responsible for his crimes because he is a product of heredity and environment, then it follows that science itself is simply the product of heredity and environment. Everyone must remember the story of the murderer who said in court: "You can't blame me; it was my heredity and environment that caused me to kill" and the judge who replied, "It is my heredity and environment that sentences you to hang by the neck until dead."

Those who deny freedom of the will always except themselves. There are, of course, men who have lost their reason; but to argue that crime itself is a loss of reason is to deny the freedom of the will and to deny that is to deny the specific nature of man as having reason. Freedom is the first property of reason. It is everywhere, always present in it. To deny the one you must deny the other; if you say that man is morally irresponsible, you must conclude that he is irrational — but then how could you conclude? Everyone knows from personal experience that when he does wrong he does wrong. You cannot deny first principles without denying common sense. Determinists are not just wrong, they are in the proper sense of the word Fools with a capital F. They may be learned and sincere, but they deny what they affirm and are saying, sometimes loudly, clearly, and, alas, with an effective rhetoric, absolutely nothing.

Crime is not an illness, and the primary function of punishment is not medicinal but retributive. Its primary purpose is not to rehabilitate but to give someone his due. Punishment is not a medical act but a moral act; it is in the order of justice.

111

Coeducational prisons have been proposed to relieve tension and resentment. They even conducted an opinion poll at Leavenworth and found an unsurprising preponderance of agreement with the theory. I know nothing about running prisons; I am talking about the philosophy of punishment on the level of principles that are certain. However you run prisons, they must hurt. That is the point. On the level of amateur opinion derived from the study of history and literature, I think we nowadays put too much stress on mere confinement as a form of punishment and would do better to admit man's immediate sentient nature. It would hurt more directly in proportion to most crimes if you put a man in the stocks or dunked him in the river like the Puritans, or gave him castor oil or forty whacks like Mussolini. We put most criminals in jail just to keep them out of our way rather than seriously facing up to what we owe them. Public ridicule, shame, dishonor, and disgrace are punishments to anyone not so far gone as to have lost self-respect.

The rehabilitator who tells the criminal he is sick, not really guilty, who says society is the cause of crime, has not disproved reality. Reality will out. Morality will out. The criminal released from a sense of his own guilt will not lose his sense of justice; he will simply blame someone else — blame the society that put him in the ghetto or the slum. You have not eliminated guilt but misplaced it. You have turned him loose with a burning thirst for a misapplied justice. The most conspicuous criminal element in America today operates exactly on that principle: they steal, rape, riot, and destroy out of a powerful disordered desire for retribution. And I am amused when not frightened at the pharisaical self-righteousness of those who say there is no crime among us. If there were no crime, they would have no reason for their fierce indignation at those of us who say there is.

All this applies to war. As Plato said, the state is the soul writ large. This means that there is an analogy between justice among persons and among nations. The primary purpose of war is retributive justice — punishment inflicted on nations that have injured innocent victims. War is therefore certainly not a crime but a very great good; war is an act of justice and soldiers are heroic men than whom the Scripture says no man hath greater love, because they lay down their lives for their friends.

A popular film has publicized the remark of General Patton to his troops: "You have heard there is no greater glory than to give your life for your country; I say, get the enemy to give his life for *his* country!" There is some good in the remark because love is not something less than justice but something more; therefore, if you love your enemy, you will see to it that he gets justice. It is not against justice that we love our neighbor as ourselves. When we see him set upon by thieves, we rush to his defense. The good Samaritan must even love the thieves and, if he does, must make them pay the penalty.

Pacifism is international sentimentalism — and it is most definitely not Christian. Particular religious sects such as the Mennonites and Quakers are special cases that come under the rule of clerical privilege: certain men may set themselves aside from the ordinary duties of society in order to pursue some higher aim that is not against the nature of society. Toleration under the rule of conscientious objection is a luxury a healthy nation can afford. But Christianity is not an idea, a theory, or a special privilege. It is a fact. And the fact remains that the history of Christian nations has been continuously military. Christian pacifists have got to deny the universal actual practice of two thousand years of Christianity, and beyond history to eternity with the wars of thrones and dominations, principalities and powers. "War is hell," said Sherman; and hell by exact theological analogy is a place of just punishment forever.

Christian pacifists begin by denying the good of war and end by rewriting Scripture so as to exclude the good of hell. Even more absurd is the case of Cassius Clay, the prizefighter who was a conscientious objector, he said, because he was a Moslem. Mohammed as pacifist, that really is the greatest! Collegiate Hindu pacifism is a joke as well: the *Bhagavad Gita* is precisely a refutation of pacifism; it is a war song in which the god Krishna explains to a reluctant prince that he must fight even against his own brothers. All the great religions of the world agree; humanity itself with one voice cries out for justice. Only sentimentalists who refuse to read their own or anyone else's Scriptures confuse peace with moral disorder, and turning the other cheek with permitting injustice when it can be stopped.

The apostasy of Christian ministers and priests in preaching this false gospel is a scandal of the age and inexcusable because it takes no great theological subtlety to know better. From a thousand clear and easily available texts in the mainstream of Christian tradition, both Protestant and Catholic, let me take just one of the most obvious and

113

best: St. Thomas Aquinas in his treatise on Charity in the *Summa Theologica*: Question 40, *De Bello* — "On War." Note that war is taken as a species of Charity. The text is Matthew 5:38–39:

> Ye have heard that it hath been said, An eye for an eye, and a tooth for a tooth. But I say unto you, That ye resist not evil: but whosoever shall smite thee on thy right cheek, turn to him the other also.

St. Thomas cites his great predecessor St. Augustine, who has behind him the entire weight of apostolic and patristic authority — both Scripture and Tradition. The only conspicuous Christian pacifist among the Fathers of the Church was the heretic Tertullian. Here is what St. Thomas says:

> As the care of the commonweal is committed to those who are in authority, it is their business to watch over the commonweal of the city, kingdom, or province subject to them. And just as it is lawful for them to have recourse to the sword in defending that commonweal against internal disturbances, when they punish evildoers, according to the words of the Apostle (Romans 13: 4): "He beareth not the sword in vain; for he is God's minister, an avenger to execute wrath upon him that doeth evil"; so too, it is their business to have recourse to the sword of war in defending the commonweal against external enemies. Hence it is said to those who are in authority (Psalm 81:4): "Rescue the poor and deliver the needy out of the hand of the sinner"; and for this reason Augustine says: "The natural order conducive to peace among mortals demands that the power to declare and counsel war should be in the hands of those who hold the supreme authority." Secondly a just cause is required, namely that those who are attacked should be attacked because they deserve it on account of some fault. Wherefore Augustine says: "A just war is wont to be described as one that avenges wrongs, when a nation or state has to be punished for refusing to make amends for the wrongs inflicted by its subjects, or to restore what it has seized unjustly."

And further, referring directly to the famous verse, "Resist not evil," St. Thomas says:

> Such precepts, as Augustine observes, should always be borne in readiness of mind so that we be ready to obey them, and if necessary to refrain from resistance or self-defense. Nevertheless, it is necessary, sometimes, for a man to act otherwise for the common good, or for the good of those with whom he is fighting. Hence Augustine says: "Those whom we have to punish with a kindly severity, it is necessary to handle in many ways against their will. For when we are stripping a man of the lawlessness of sin, it is good for him to be vanquished, since nothing is more hopeless than the happiness of sinners, whence arises a guilty impunity and an evil will, like an internal enemy."
>
> Those who wage war justly aim at peace and so they are not opposed to peace, except to "the evil peace which Our Lord came not to send upon earth" (Matthew 10:34). Hence Augustine says, "We do not seek peace in order to be at war, but we go to war that we may have peace. Be peaceful therefore in warring, so that you may vanquish those whom you war against and bring them to the prosperity of peace."

A great and final execution of this precept "resist not evil" comes from Christ Himself when the legitimate authority of Rome arrests Him. In a severe repudiation, not of war, but of lawlessness, Christ, like the pagan Socrates, goes to His death, though innocent, rather than so much as to resist the lawful authority even when it is wrong. "Put up again thy sword. For all they that take the sword, shall perish with the sword." He is talking about resisting the police, not about the police themselves. For the state "beareth not the sword in vain."

Those who today commit violent acts of civil disobedience in the name of Christ because they are against war are sorry sentimentalists at best who, St. Paul says, "cannot endure sound doctrine but heap to themselves teachers having itching ears." At worst they are the teachers.

What lawyers, judges, wardens, policemen, senators, and soldiers do in concrete instances of war and arrest depends upon their particular knowledge and practical experience. But whatever they do must be an application of these principles, given first by reason itself and carried on continuously by the broad culture of Christendom of which the nation is a part — and for that matter by all the great religions and cultures of the world. My purpose has been to wipe the slate clean of a destructive and ultimately nihilistic nonsense that has weakened the exercise of justice both at home and abroad. I mean that weak, simpering denial of the dignity of men which confuses crime with sickness, and therefore punishment and war with cruelty when they are proper instruments of charity and justice.

We have suffered in the United States these last ten years a frightening failure of nerve. Of course, there are conscious agents of the failure. In 1939 they sang the same peace songs, played on the same banjos by some of the same men. Pete Seeger was around back then, and Arlo Guthrie's father. There was an organization called The Yanks Are *Not* Coming Committee, and college students marched in protests chanting, "No sir, the Yanks are not coming!" They had all the banners and handbills printed up when the news arrived that Hitler had broken the Stalin-Hitler pact and invaded the Soviet Union. Overnight the slogan changed. And because so many banners and bills had already been printed up — why waste the money? — they simply stamped on an extra phrase: "No sir, the Yanks are not coming — *too late*! With such talent as this, antiwar is war, as Orwell said.

The entire student movement for peace was changed into a whooping propaganda binge for immediate involvement in the war, somehow to defend the United States, which had not yet been attacked. Paul Robeson sang his "Ballad for Americans" and those few who still opposed the war, like Charles Lindbergh, were called fascists. Justice, to the Left, is always and only whatever advances the Soviet Union. The pacifism of the anti-Vietnam movement was like a rerun of an old TV series. Antiwar movements are not really antiwar. They are herds of sentimentalists moved by a shrewd enemy who does not believe a word of it. The enemy wanted us to "stop the killing" in Vietnam so as to have a clean sweep of killing himself. Whatever the case may have been in Southeast Asia, whether we were right or wrong, peace is not a lack of war. It is a state of justice. It is, in St. Augustine's famous phrase, "the tranquility of order."

There is a sad malaise in America today, a failure of nerve, a lack of will. People say: "I don't want to run the world; I just want to go home." There is doubt about the justness not only of our cause, but of any cause. Sentimentalism is a chorus of "Who is to say?" The question denies that men can know what is right and wrong. But somebody thinks he knows, and somebody is going to run the world. And if it is run by criminals, we will learn to know the difference too — too late.

Do the boys come home? What is home? If punishment is wrong, they must all come home even from the highways and the crossroads — the police must come home. If the enemy is at the door, we must retreat to the bedroom and presumably "make love, not war." Shall we console ourselves as they drive us in chains to the workgangs and the concentration camps that there are no cowards because there is no shame? To use an old, true cliché, history is like a relay race — and we are the ones who failed to carry the baton. Ours is the first shame in the history of the United States. To be beaten, having fought, is poetry, as at Troy or Roncesvalles, from which future courage springs; but this is the war we walked away from because we failed to believe our cause is just. Whose is, then — theirs? Or have we sunk below the level of civilized behavior and said: We are a people who do not believe that any cause is just, who do not believe in justice? Ours is the generation about whom it will not be said that "this was their finest hour" but that they went home. And this is the way the United States ends — not the world, because the Communists win — not with a bang but a whimper. When archaeologists one day dig in our burnt rubble, they will find thousands of broken ping-pong balls.

Justice is not *given;* justice is something we must deserve. Robert Frost was very much mistaken in his homely remarks about home. "Home," the woman in "The Death of the Hired Man" says, "is the place you somehow haven't to deserve," the place, her husband says, "Where, when you go there, they have to take you in." The whole Christian tradition has taught a much higher view of home — that home was something to defend even to the death. Justice is something we very much have to deserve, and to do that we must not only change but change direction, get hold of ourselves, purify the wells, drink some long, cool draughts of healthy principle. "Blessed are those who hunger and thirst after justice." And "blessed are the merciful" — the ones who in charity are willing to sacrifice themselves beyond justice in giving their lives so that justice will be done.

8 The Risk of Certainty

How quaint it seems to look back now at 1941, when "the hand that held the dagger struck," in Roosevelt's phrase, and when an Anglican bishop mobilized New York against a well-known immoralist. "What is to be said of colleges and universities," he wrote,

> which hold up before our youth as a responsible teacher or philosopher . . . a man who is a recognized propagandist against both religion and morality, and who specifically defends adultery . . . . There are those who are so confused morally and mentally that they see nothing wrong in the appointment . . . of one who in his published writings said, "Outside of human desires there is no moral standard."

As a result of this attack, the most famous philosopher in the world was dismissed from a professorship at City College on two legal technicalities and a third count that really strikes at the heart of the matter. Judge McGeehan, in his decision, quoted passages from Bertrand Russell's books advocating behavior contrary to the New York Penal Law and argued that a man who had published such opinions was not morally fit to instruct youth. According to the law,

> a person who entices an unmarried female of any age of previous chaste character to any place for the purpose of sexual intercourse is guilty of abduction, [and] rape [includes any] act of sexual intercourse with a female not his wife under the age of eighteen years.

In *Education and the Modern World* Russell had written:

I am sure that university life would be better, both intellectually and morally, if most university students had temporary childless marriages. This would provide a solution to the sexual urge.

And in *Marriage and Morals* he said:

For my part, while I am quite convinced that companionate marriage would be a step in the right direction and would do a great deal of good, I do not think that it goes far enough. I think that all sex relations which do not involve children should be regarded as a purely private affair, and that if a man and a woman choose to live together without having children, that should be no one's business but their own. I should not hold it desirable that either a man or a woman should enter upon the serious business of a marriage intended to lead to children without having had previous experience.

What Russell means by "companionate marriage," which he says does not "go far enough," is clearly included under the legal definition of abduction and, since some college students are under eighteen, it is included under the legal definition of rape as well. The judge concludes:

Assuming that Mr. Russell could teach for two years in City College without promulgating the doctrines which he seems to find necessary to spread on the printed pages at frequent intervals, his appointment violates a perfectly obvious canon of pedagogy, namely, that the personality of the teacher has more to do with forming a student's opinion than many syllogisms . . . . Academic freedom does not mean academic license. It is the freedom to do good and not to teach evil. Academic freedom cannot authorize a teacher to teach that murder or treason are good. Nor can it permit a teacher to teach directly or indirectly that sexual intercourse between students, where the female is under the age of eighteen years, is proper.

This is not a voice "hoarse from long disuse" from the Dark Ages or even from the age of Queen Victoria, but a New York court as recently as 1941. The law and the interpretation of the law were both against what thirty years later has become an establishment of vice. To defend Russell in 1941, they had to weasel words. Paul Edwards, for example, in an appendix to Russell's book *Why I Am Not A Christian*, says,

> It is not true that Russell, either in the passages quoted by the Judge or anywhere else, *encouraged* adultery. What Russell maintains is, firstly, that sexual relations between unmarried people are not morally wrong if they have sufficient affection for each other and that this is a purely private matter in which the state should take no interest. . . . This is not at all the same thing as "encouraging" adultery. If anything, Russell's advocacy of legalized companionate marriage may be regarded as an argument against adultery.

Companionate marriage is fornication — what an argument against adultery! It comes under the New York definition of abduction and, if arranged for persons under eighteen, of rape. Poor Edwards says that Russell's notorious nudism was really in support of decency because the human body is a decent thing; that his published opinions about self-abuse and unspeakable vice show him to be really in support of normality. Russell writes about the latter in *Portraits from Memory:*

> If two adults voluntarily enter such a relation this is a matter which concerns them only, and in which, therefore, the community ought not to intervene. . . . If it were still believed, as it once was, that the toleration of such behavior would expose the community to the fate of Sodom and Gommorah, the community would have every right to intervene merely on the ground that such conduct is thought wicked.

In his peroration, Edwards cries that Russell's "reputation and livelihood were at stake," and that the trial was a form of character assassination working hardship on a great and innocent man. A scant eight printed lines further, he reports Russell's triumphant entry into Harvard, then Columbia, his receiving the Order of Merit from George VI and the Nobel Prize. Reputation and livelihood be damned — one of the richest and most successful careers of the century was created out of just such public scandals as the one at City College.

In 1941 the people of New York, aroused by Bishop Manning and protected by the Superior Court, made a defense of morality against a man who had been, beyond the shadow of a doubt, as the Bishop said, "a recognized propagandist against both religion and morality and who specifically defends adultery." Thirty-odd years ago the people of a sophisticated city refused to take the public insult of Russell's appointment to their college. Would anyone today?

Russell was a clever man who knew most of the other famous clever men of his day. He was a marvelous raconteur with a reputation for mathematical genius. But Russell as a teacher of philosophy, forming the young, impressionable minds of college students — that was once upon a very recent time unthinkable. Free to speak and write; free to express his opinions, no matter how bizarre; to eat nothing but vegetables, or to parade on the Atlantic City boardwalk in the nude — yes. But not to occupy a position of the highest intellectual and moral authority, even with his clothes on. Once upon a time we freely granted such a person the right to publish books, to lecture at City Hall, harangue the mob at Union Square, and, under the auspices of a correctly labeled forum, to lecture on college campuses as an extracurricular affair. We should have been, in fact, positively sorry to see him absent from the Sunday supplements along with Mahatma Gandhi, Charles Atlas, and the grape-cure folk. But today it is illegal to teach morality, and Christians have been forbidden to teach in public schools.

The Conde Nast publishing company would not ordinarily be cited in an essay on pornography; they publish family magazines like *House and Garden*. But they also market slick fiction and photography in the guise of a fashion magazine called *Vogue*, and another for "the smart young woman" called *Mademoiselle*, which I shall take as a fair sample of the moral level we have sunk to in the single generation since Russell's triumphal entry into Harvard.

What should we expect from a fashion magazine especially addressed to college girls, some of whom, at least, are still below the age

121

set by New York law as vulnerable to statutory rape? In the first place, the magazine consists almost entirely of advertisements for clothes — as might be expected; but also — as might be expected but ought not to be — the appeal is not to serious young ladies thinking of the classroom or even the junior prom. As if the expressionistic leers out of *The Blue Angel* on the pinched and painted faces of these wretched little dolls and their tiger-striped pajamas were not enough, there is a full-page advertisement for a book called *Sex and the Single Girl* that reads as follows:

> "Theoretically, a 'nice' single woman has no sex life. What nonsense!" says Helen Brown, the author of *Sex and the Single Girl*. Her new book is the first that dares to recognize the physical as well as the emotional needs of the single woman.

Note that what the court defined as criminal offense is now a physical need. The ad goes on to list the book as containing among other things "an eye-opening discussion of virginity — its problems and its future." And, further, the college girl is told in this issue of a fashion magazine entirely dedicated to her that

> being single today is vastly different from what it was in your mother's day. [That, thirty years ago, was Russell's day, when mother went to college.] The single career woman is today's new glamour girl. . . . She can do *what* she wants to *when* she wants. She answers to nobody for her actions, her decisions, her behavior. She can have a marvelous unburdened, exciting time during these years. And that's exactly what Helen Brown shows you how to do in this bouyant joyful guide to living single in superlative style.

Well, "she answers to nobody" and the sad thing is, if that is so, that nobody will ever answer to her.

Among the testimonial blurbs is one from a certain Dr. Ellis:

> Faces up to the problem of premarital sex relations with refreshing candor. The discussion of the single girl and her premarital affairs is unusual for its honesty and realism.

122

The very cant Judge Woolsey used in the *Ulysses* case in 1933 —
"honesty and realism."

But all this so far is only in the advertising pages. The lead article
for the smart young mademoiselle is called "Lady Chatterley Goes to
College." The caption reads: "What do students say about the new
morality? What kind of a girl has an affair in college, and why?" Now
such an article as this, which purports to tell young girls about the
doings of the style-setters, must propagandize for the behavior it
describes. Reporting in such a case is a form of saying "everybody's
doing it," which in a fashion magazine is a command.

> Students do not yet talk openly about the new morality.
> They fight for what they want indirectly. Editorials in
> campus papers plumping for later curfews or freedom to
> entertain in dormitory rooms are couched in high-
> sounding language to disguise the fact that at bottom the
> issue is sex. But sex it really is.

This is, if not refreshing, at least candid admission of hypocrisy about
"freedom" and "tolerance." Behind the Liberal slogans, according to
this article, lies sex. Actually it is the other way around: the campus
editorials and the protests do not exist for sex; sex is deliberately
exacerbated — by articles just like this — for the sake of the protests.
Poor mademoiselle is vexed to nightmare by the English reading lists
and what purports to be psychological and sociological analysis. Poor
little things are shamed into prurience, finally to become like men —
to dress in men's clothes and read his smut, try his careers, spit on her
hands, swing a baseball bat, become a doctor, engineer, photographer
— anything but what she is. "Public morality," the article goes on,

> is obviously having a set-to with private morality. . . .
> Not only are a great many students Doing It (about a
> fourth of all undergraduate women, more at certain col-
> leges), but that more and more Do It all the time.

An academic journal reports, according to the article, that "the old
goal, chastity until marriage, has been replaced by a new one, chastity
until engagement," and it quotes one authority on premarital intercourse who believes the coming standard is "sexual permissiveness
when affection exists." And so we have Russell's companionate mar-

riage word for word according to his dictum that morality is desire. And there is no mistake about "encouragement," or where this article appears and for what purpose. It is in a magazine that sets the fashion for college girls and it is plainly written with the intention of selling young girls this "new morality." It proceeds to report on what it says is the behavior of girls at the "best" colleges, proving the contention by quotations from fiction written by recent graduates. The heroine of one story called "Sentimental Education," a title taken from Flaubert, is a "pink-cheeked Radcliffe girl" who has an "affair" with a Harvard boy.

> And why do Caroline and Elgin sleep together? Is it because of the bomb or for some complicated reason? No, it is because of good-natured lust. Elgin begins to think seriously of girls when his roommate, Dimitri, starts bringing a girl called Felicia to the room. He notices Caroline because he is thinking about love (the reading for his literature and history courses is full of detailed accounts of passion. . . .) He sees her first on the steps of the Widener Library, surely one of the richest caches for such books in the world.

The young aristocracy at Harvard, catching reechy kisses in a fitting place — the stacks; disciplined in loveless sex. Not sex learned secretly in washrooms or from peddlers of postcards on summer workshops in Venice, but from ordinary class assignments, from texts purchased over the counter at college bookstores, read, analyzed, and discussed in seminars — "Detailed accounts of passion." For example, one of the college classics is Faulkner's *Sanctuary*, where an impotent gangster commits rape with a corncob. In Proust's *Remembrance of Things Past*, one lesbian performs upon another underneath the portrait of her father, on which she spits at the end of the encounter; and in another passage famous in the seminars for its "Dickensian" effect, a masochist is beaten with chains to satisfy, one supposes, a "physical and emotional need," or even a "basic human function."

Students read these books, and worse ones, on assignment, along with arguments from the Liberal philosophers like Russell. Add to this the magazines like *Mademoiselle*, the anthropology lectures on the ways of the Samoans, and the movies, and you have what amounts to a powerful, and for young people almost irresistible, compulsion to specific suicide — I mean the destruction of the species in despair of love and marriage.

This much must be admitted by the Liberal reader if any has read this far: (1) The classics of modern literature — not under-the-counter pornography but the works of Joyce, Gide, Proust, Faulkner, Lawrence, Mann, and many others — are not "honest, forthright, realistic" works depicting the lives of "real people." It must be clearly understood that if you want to defend these works, you must defend them as they are and not abstractly transform them into a debater's fiction. You must defend as good the encouragement of immorality and the dissemination of detailed, exciting information on how to practice it. And if you defend these books, you have got to defend the results. If you defend the teaching of these books, you have got to defend the immoral practices of students, if not yourself, who proceed to the further question *Mademoiselle* asks: "Whether the colleges should provide students with information about contraceptives." Of course, they get the things, not just the information now, in junior high school.

There is a gross abuse of the doctrine of the Golden Mean that would have us strike a middle ground between truth and error, as if when Professor X said two plus two are four and Professor Y that they are six, we should amicably settle for five. We must distinguish contraries, between which there is a mean, from contradictories, between which there is none. According to the powerful proposition at the beginning of philosophy with which Plato and Aristotle refuted sophistry, man is *not* "the measure of all things"; things measure men, and therefore truth is not a matter of opinion, nor force the arbiter of argument.

The currently established academic religion has as its first principle the axiom that no proposition may be held with such certitude as to exclude its contradictory. It is a doctrine dogmatically defined and adhered to with a ferocious emotional commitment, so that one is not opposed so much as anathematized if he steps outside its lines. If we contend — to take a literary example — according to the definitions of Aristotle, (1) that poetry is the imitation of men in action, (2) that free moral choice is a property necessarily, everywhere, and always present in rationality, and conclude *ergo* (3) that poetry is moral — so far

125

the argument is unexceptionable. Everyone has a right to his own opinion, even Aristotle. However, if we go the one step further and apply the principle to particular cases, they say we "go too far." If we say James Joyce's *Ulysses* is a bad novel because it exhibits immoral men in action as good, we are told that we have substituted diatribe for literary analysis. And if we add that an immersion in such representations of sick and immoral behavior damages the sensibilities, they call us cultural McCarthyites because, as Newman said, "They are sure to say we carry things too far when we carry them home to themselves."

The university, like Naples, is situated between the Eden of Campania and the Vesuvian fires of hell. In the groves of academe one looks from the level lawns of his Aristotle to scan the student reading lists or accidentally hears a lecture down the hall — and it is so noisome. To go down fighting Achilles, or even Attila the Hun, is one thing, but to fight the *New York Times Book Review* takes more than a heart or even a stomach; it takes a superhuman patience of the intellect.

A criticism based on Aristotle cannot be dismissed as moral diatribe. Nor can moral diatribe based on the criticism be dismissed either. The critic who puts moral considerations first because morality is "the first property of man" cannot be told that unless he argues from the position to the contrary, he is a bigot. Not only would that be illiberal, it would be fantastic — a betrayal of literature and the academy as well. Moral questions must be raised, and if someone disagrees with a moral judgment, he must submit moral reasons for his disagreement. A generation ago T. S. Eliot boldly if belatedly ushered English literature into the twentieth century to the tune of Dryden's song:

> 'Tis well an old age is out
> And time to begin a new.

It is time again. Prophetic yawns have turned once more to the yawn they started from. One more Rimbaud and we shall die of boredom; another shocking film, experimental novel or theology, and we shall expire in the millennial ho-hum. The cultural epoch introduced by Baudelaire a hundred years ago now runs its course, monotonously in circles like an auto race. Its best effort was a vain attempt by men of considerable genius to make art into religion, and its worst has been beneath contempt. Many think the world is coming to an end because it is certain now that Modernism will end. Never fear. The world has miles to go before it sleeps.

Newman gave a sermon at St. Mary's, Oxford on the text: "They say unto Him, We are able." When the mother of Zebedee's sons had asked that they sit to the right and left of Our Lord in His Kingdom, He replied: "Are ye able to drink of the cup that I shall drink of, and to be baptized with the baptism that I am baptized with?" And they said: "We are able."

Newman interprets these words to mean that "if . . . faith be the essence of a Christian life . . . it follows that our duty lies in risking upon Christ's word what we have, for what we have not." And then he makes an application of this rule, so simple yet surprising as to make us almost afraid:

> I dare say that what I have said as yet seems plain and unexceptionable to most of those who hear me; yet sure, when I proceed to draw the practical inference which immediately follows, there are those who in their secret hearts draw back. Men allow us Ministers of Christ to proceed in our preaching, while we confine ourselves to the general truths, until they see that they themselves are implicated in them, and have to act upon them; and then they suddenly come to a stand . . . . There is no truth, however overpoweringly clear, but men may escape from it by shutting their eyes: there is no duty, however urgent, but they may find ten thousand good reasons against it in their own case. And they are sure to say we carry things too far when we carry them home to themselves. Consider for an instant. Let every one who hears me ask himself the questions, what stake has he in the truth of Christ's promise? How would he be a whit worse off, supposing (which is impossible) but supposing it to fail? . . . What have we ventured for Christ?

The word "adventure" derives from the Latin *venire*, "to come." The same root gives us "venture" as in "nothing ventured, nothing gained," and "Advent," the season of Christ's coming. What is an adventure? It is a putting of oneself forward to meet the unexpected, the risking of what we have in favor of what we might have, the known in favor of the unknown, staking something on the future — life itself put to the chance of disaster and success. To invite the unexpected is often to meet with disappointments; to go for the unknown may be to lose the known. When we read adventure stories in the safety of our pipe and slippers, the chair becomes uneasy; we draw closer to the comfortable familiar fire, feeling for the moment, in our imaginations, a delightful chill from the frozen empty spaces. But the Christian life is a real adventure and the call to it a question: as if you were a businessman who put his savings in a merchant ship, you must ask, "Suppose the ship goes down? How much have I ventured that I might lose if Christianity were false? My possessions? My career? My life? Or have I prudently invested in the world as well, so that if heaven fails, at least I shall have had a successful time below? How many diamonds have I sewn into the hem of my spiritual jacket? How many accounts in religious Swiss banks?"

Newman goes on to explain what is implicit in the promise James and John so rashly made, who — not knowing what Christ meant, but only that He meant it — replied so quickly to His question, "We are able." James was the first of the Apostles to be martyred, while John remained, at the end of a long life, the last. It was he who, as Newman says,

> had to bear a length of years in loneliness, exile, and
> weakness. . . . Well might so great a Saint say, at the end
> of his days, Come, Lord Jesus Christ, as those who are
> weary of the night, and wait for the morning.

It is said that Christianity, if it is to survive, must face the modern world, must come to terms with the way things are in the sense of the current drift of things. It is just the other way around: If we are to survive, we must face Christianity. The strongest reactionary force impeding progress is the cult of progress itself, which, cutting us off from our roots, makes growth impossible and choice unnecessary. We expire in the lazy, utterly helpless drift, the spongy warmth of an absolute uncertainty. Where nothing is ever true, or right or wrong, there are no problems; where life is meaningless we are free from responsibility, the way a slave or scavenger is free. Futility breeds carelessness, against which stands the stark alternative: against the radical uncertainty by which modern man has lived — as in a game of Russian roulette, stifled in the careless "now" between the click and the explosion, living by the dull grace of empty chambers — the risk of certainty.

9 The Emperor of Ice Cream

The eighteenth-century satirist Lawrence Sterne ridicules the common religion of his day in his novel *Tristram Shandy* when Uncle Toby says, in the name of a wise, benign, thoroughly British tolerance, "My Church is the best Church because it never interferes with a man's politics or his religion." In the eighteenth century, after three hundred years of war, men were ready to settle for something less than truth; governments were to be founded by "social contract" rather than Divine Right and individuals to love one another by a set of conventions known as "good manners." It was of nations as Alexander Pope said of a certain lady:

> Virtue she finds too painful an endeavor
> Content to dwell in decencies forever.

Weary from the theological wars of the preceding three hundred years, polite society reduced religion from a reality of the mind and heart, for which one must fight to win or die, to a "sensibility" whose seat was more often than not the tongue, because men made a "profession" of what they really did not believe. Their hearts were in their mouths. As for dying, that was impolite — as a famous dying lady said, "Please do not disturb the guests." Their slogan was not "seeing is believing," which might have been true for Galileo and the men of the Renaissance, but "saying is believing" — that is, belief is a matter of what people say.

Voltaire, expressing the extreme of eighteenth-century sensibility, speaks with characteristic brilliance and malice on the popular subject of the origin of this convention known as religion: "Religion properly speaking began the day a charlatan first met a fool." The truth, according to Voltaire, is really that lie which best satisfies the prejudice of your audience. Perhaps this was more a show of cynicism for his jaded readers than a real conviction, but it reveals the common doctrine of rationalism that teaches that since there is no truth, our lives must be based upon opinion; and since men differ in opinion, a common agreement must adjudicate among us, whether by explicit contract, as in constitutional government, or by implicit assent, as in good manners; or by a church, in matters of religion, whose chief mark, as Uncle Toby says, is that it leaves well enough alone.

Newman describes this religion as it appeared in his day, one hundred years later:

> There is in the literary world just now an affectation of calling religion a "sentiment"; and it must be confessed that usually it is nothing more with our own people, educated or rude. Objects are barely necessary to it. I do not say so of old Calvinism or Evangelical religion . . . but these are only denominations, parties, schools, compared with the national religion of England in its length and breadth. "Bible religion" is both the recognized title and the best description of English religion. It consists not in rites or creeds, but mainly in having the Bible read in Church, in the family and in private. Now I am far indeed from undervaluing that mere knowledge of Scripture which is imparted to the population thus promiscuously . . . it has to a certain point made up for great and grievous losses in its Christianity. It has given them a high moral standard . . . [and] so far has been of service; but still, much more is necessary . . . to answer to the idea of a religion . . . . It is not a religion of persons and things, of acts of faith and of direct devotion; but of sacred scenes and pious sentiments . . . . Its doctrines are not so much facts as stereotyped aspects of facts; and it is afraid, so to say, of walking around them. It induces its followers to be content with this meagre view of revealed truth; or, rather, it is suspicious and protests, or is frightened as if it saw a figure move out of its frame, when Our Lord, the Blessed Virgin, or the Holy Apostles are spoken of as real beings.

131

This is not a criticism by one denomination of another; but of the general drift of all Christianity, which suffers from a common disease of the imagination. No matter how much we profess, the facts of Christianity are not real to us because nothing is real to us. We have come to doubt the very existence of reality.

What had been a mere slipshod sentimentality in Uncle Toby's day was formulated and defined as the established religion of England and America a century later and called Liberalism. Its theologians and philosophers count among them some of the most famous men and women of letters in the nineteenth century: John Stuart Mill, George Eliot, Herbert Spencer, Matthew Arnold. Mill's *Essay on Liberty* is better known by college students today than the Sermon on the Mount; it is studied as a model of rhetoric in composition, as a model of argument in logic, as a model of wisdom in political science. And yet its major contention is false and self-contradictory: since truth, it says, is nothing more than opinion, each and every opinion must be equally respected as having the rights of truth. Therefore, no one can establish anything so certainly as to exclude the possible truth of its contradictory. Whatever you think, you may be wrong, because the ground of all reality has been rejected and there is nothing to measure the intellect against. The intellect is no longer regarded as naturally tending toward truth. *Intellectus natura sua non ad verum tendit*, says the new Liberal scholasticism. Like Hamlet, our wills are puzzled and we have lost the name of action.

In the twentieth century the doctrine of Liberalism has perfected its tendency and in advanced circles today the Bible is of course not read at all. That fact alone should shock anyone with a sense of history. The one book all men have read, whose imagery, ideas, and very language were the sun that held the planetary system of Christendom in order, is not now read; and one of the secondary consequences is that nothing else in English literature before 1920 can be read without copious footnotes. And we now hear, not that whatever we think *may* be wrong — which was the agnostic position of a hundred years ago — but absolutely, according to the doctrine of a dogmatic Liberalism, that it *must* be wrong. There is *no* truth and *every* belief is an error. Although it is obviously self-contradictory, there is abroad today a dogmatic and inquisitorial Liberalism that insists on the positive establishment of disbelief, that proposes an infidelity at the point of the sword. Matthew Arnold, who in his essays professes a Christian Liberalism, in his prophetic poems voices more plainly and powerfully his deepest conviction of Modernistic despair, loosed from the sack of nineteenth century Liberalism like Odysseus' evil winds:

> The Sea of Faith
> Was once, too, at the full, and round earth's shore
> Lay like the fold of a bright girdle furled.
> But now I only hear
> Its melancholy, long, withdrawing roar,
> Retreating, to the breath
> Of the night wind down the vast edges drear
> And naked shingles of the world.

This is the voice of the wilderness crying in the universities. It is the voice of Yeats' "beast"—

> Moving its slow thighs, while all about it
> Reel shadows of the indignant desert birds.

It is in the bitter resignation of Thomas Hardy, whose unsentimental pacifism is not based upon a mistaken view of love of one's neighbor but a conviction of the hopelessness of any conviction worth fighting for:

> Hodge the drummer never knew,
> Fresh from his Wessex home,
> The meaning of the broad carew,
> The stars, the dusty loam,
> and why uprose to nightly view
> Strange stars amid the gloom.

And A. E. Housman's stiffer-lipped despair:

> The gale it plies the saplings double,
> It blows so hard 'twill soon be gone,
> Today the Roman and his trouble
> Are ashes under Uricon.

And even in a timbre willfully misunderstood like that of the happy rustic Frost:

And lonely as it is, that loneliness
Will be more lonely ere it will be less —
A blanker whiteness of benighted snow
With no expression, nothing to express.

Or —

Some say the world will end in fire
Some say ice.

Pass over, as the rhetoricians say, the obvious in Eliot, Pound, Auden, and the French from Baudelaire to Valéry. Voltaire believed significance derived from a man-made reason, and therefore reduced Christianity to an unreasonable convention that really ought to go. The Romantics declared significance to be emotional and reduced Christianity to a sentiment. Wordsworth said:

I felt the sentiment of Being spread
O'er all that moves and all that seemeth still;
O'er all that, lost beyond the reach of thought
And human knowledge, to the human eye
Invisible, yet liveth to the heart . . . .

Modernists, repudiating both reason and affection, repudiating the idea of significance itself, have dispensed with Christianity except as a metaphor:

And the world which seems
To lie before us like a land of dreams
Hath really neither joy, nor love, nor light,
Nor certitude . . . .

What argument can possibly suffice to one who exercises neither reason nor emotion? What can be said to, say, Bertrand Russell, if he really does believe that reason is a construct the purpose of which is to free us "from our fellow-man, free us from the petty planet on which our bodies impotently crawl?" What can be said to Wallace Stevens if imagination *is* reality and "the only Emperor is the Emperor of Ice Cream?"

134

The *Summa Theologica* contains clear refutations of reasonable heresies but scarcely touches anyone who disbelieves in the very difference between truth and error. It has become now a matter of civil rights to allow that two plus two are five, dogmatically anathema that two plus two are four, illegal to insist that "stones are hard and water wet," that Britain is an island, Elizabeth its Queen, and that Eve was made from Adam's rib and therefore women must be subject to their husbands and their husbands must love their wives. In a world where lady preachers, unlike walking dogs, have left the circus, and where anything may be asserted except the truth, argument is futile. We have the lawyer's brief in the *Summa Theologica*, but where are the twelve good men and true?

Newman discovered, in his own experience first, then in the Bible and in history, that God is not an argument — thank God. His case is a matter of flesh and blood. All of which is nothing new; in fact it is the revival of the oldest cliché in Christendom. But the importance is not the discovery in the abstract. It is rather that this man really did discover it. Newman did not merely write down a true proposition; he had the personal experience of conversion, the "turning around" and seeing in faith the truth. According to the "Bible religion" of the day, everyone believed, in a sense, that Jesus loved him because the Bible told him so. But Newman saw the pictures in the frame begin to move. In future years the "higher" critics will contend that Newman never really existed. They will say he was a literalized personification of conversion, of putting on the "new man."

His is the oldest kind of apologetics — not so much an argument as a presentation. "What is truth?" says jesting Pilate. Newman points — *There* is truth, Who says: "This is my Body, this is my Blood." If God is Christ, and Christ is truth, then truth is a person to be believed in, not an idea. *Credo in Deum*, not *Credo quod Deus sit*. Propositions may *have* truth but to *be* truth is to be a person; and to know truth is therefore *cognoscere*, not *scire*. This is the experience behind Newman's misunderstood, and perhaps deliberately distorted, distinction between notional and real knowledge. Newman does not attack Aristotle and St. Thomas, nor is he an integral personalist who thinks creeds and dogmatic definitions are mere leaven in the rising bread of left-wing political panaceas. He is defending dogma against the sociologizing of religion. Nor have Dulles and Kueng (Mr. William Marshner in an understatement has called the latter a "philosophical imbecile") any right to appropriate Newman's theory of development in support of their materialist evolutionism. Here is what Newman says in the celebrated passage from the *Grammar of Assent:*

> Science gives us the grounds or premises from which religious truths are to be inferred; but it does not set about inferring them, much less does it reach the inference — that is not its province. It brings before us phenomena, and it leaves us, if we will, to call them works of design, wisdom, or benevolence; and further still, if we will, to proceed to confessing an intelligent Creator. We have to take its facts, and to give them a meaning, and to draw our own conclusions from them. First comes knowledge, then a view, then reasoning, and then belief. This is why science has so little of a religious tendency; deductions have no power of persuasion. The heart is commonly reached, not through reason, but through the imagination, by means of direct impressions, by the testimony of facts and events, by history, by description. Persons influence us, voices melt us, looks subdue us, deeds inflame us. Many a man will live and die upon a dogma; no man will be a martyr for a conclusion.

And he goes on:

> A conclusion is but an opinion; it is not a thing which is, which we are "quite certain about"; and . . . no one, I say, will die for his own calculations: he dies for realities . . . . I have no confidence, then, in philosophers who cannot help being religious, and are Christians by implication. They sit at home, and reach forward to distances which astonish us; but they hit without grasping, and are sometimes as confident about shadows as about realities. They have worked out by a calculation the lie of a country which they never saw, and mapped it by means of a gazetteer; and, like blind men, though they can put a stranger on his way, they cannot walk straight themselves, and do not feel it quite their business to walk at all . . . . Tell men to gain notions of a Creator from His

works, and, if they were to set about it (which nobody does) they would be jaded and wearied by the labyrinth they were tracing. . . . To most men argument makes the point in hand only more doubtful, and considerably less impressive. . . . Life is not long enough for a religion of inferences; we shall never have done beginning if we determine to begin with proof. We shall ever be laying foundations, we shall turn theology into evidences, and divines into textuaries. We shall never get at our first principles. Resolve to believe nothing, and you must prove your proofs . . . sinking further and further till you come to the broad bosom of skepticism. . . . Now I wish to state all this as matter of fact . . . and if it be such we must resign ourselves to it as best we may, unless we take refuge in the intolerable paradox that the mass of men are created for nothing and are meant to leave life as they entered it.

This is Newman's one apologia and he never departs from it. It is the single lesson of his life. Everything he wrote is simply an application of its truth to circumstance. When a low Anglican controversialist attacked his conversion as a Machiavellian feint, Newman replied not with an argument but with his most famous work, a kind of autobiography. You say, Mr. Kingsley, such and such about what I have said and done. My answer? Not a lawyer's brief. Nothing about the Hotel Ritz or the night of January 13th. Rather: This is the man I am. This is my body, and my blood. And in theological controversy, where the issue was not himself and what he did, but the Church, Newman had applied the same tool of persuasion: You say the Church said such and such in 325, such and such to the contrary in 1845. Newman's reply is his greatest work, *An Essay on the Development of Christian Doctrine*, a kind of biography of the Church, an *Apologia pro Ecclesia Sua*. You offer such and such arguments against the Church, but this is she "bright as the sun, terrible as an army in battle array." Her proof is history.

Newman's position is this: Conceptual truth is extracted by the intellect from the ground of the imagination. But the modern world suffers from a disease of the imagination, so that there is no point in arguing with anyone about what God is or even whether He is until men have been able to imagine Him. When someone says of a dear friend that he has done some shameful thing, you simply say, "But you don't know the man. If you knew him, you would not believe it for a moment." Steadily, step by step, over the last few hundred years since the triumph of Rationalism and Liberalism and now Modernism, the person of Christ has been withdrawn from our experience. Generations now grow up in a religious vacuum, in an atmosphere charged, as it were, with His absence. It is no wonder that He is not known and that His name can be used as if it were any old thing in vulgar musical comedies and in more vulgar musical comedies pretending to be liturgies in churches. In such a world God is not real and nothing can be proved.

Yet Newman found a way. Take, for example, his case against one of the founding fathers of Liberalism, David Hume. Christianity, Newman says, rests on a fact. Hume does not attack the fact itself — that is, he does not replace what he considers to be the false fact with the true one; rather, he denies the antecedent credibility of the fact. He tries to sap the whole thing from beneath. He does not present Christ's bones as concrete proof that the Resurrection is a lie. No witness is called. No bone is offered as Exhibit A. He does not give evidence at all but rather attacks the validity of sight. I do not say that this miracle did not take place, he argues, but that miracles are *per se* incredible — and therefore I will not so much as look at your evidence or listen to the testimony of your witnesses. Newman explains the position by quoting Hume's own words:

> It is argued by Hume against the actual occurrence of the Jewish and Christian miracles that, whereas, "it is experience only which gives authority to human testimony, and it is the same experience which assures us of the laws of nature," therefore "when these two kinds of experience are contrary" to each other "we are bound to subtract the one from the other"; and, in consequence, since we have no experience of the violation of natural laws, and much experience of a violation of truth, "we may establish it as a maxim that no human testimony can have such force as to prove a miracle, and make it a just foundation for any such system of religion."

All right, how can we reply? With witnesses? But Hume has just cut

138

the ground from the very idea of testimony! Nor would signs and wonders move him; were Our Lord Himself to stand before him and say, "Put your hand into my side," he would maintain the antecedent incredibility of even his own fingers. No witness can be trusted because men either lie or are mistaken, whereas the laws of nature are constant. Every Christian, if he thinks, must sooner or later meet this argument, though he seldom finds it formulated so intelligently. Hume is not Voltaire; he argues for the sake of neither wit nor malice. Newman's reply is at once personal and perfect and, once we see it, turns out to be the commonest one we ever had, common both to the Church and to schoolboys.

Newman does not reply at all, he "retorts," that is, he "twists" the argument back upon its advocate. Newman has one real answer to all questions: "My Lord and my God." And he has one method for getting the doubter to see as Doubting Thomas saw. So now with Hume. You say, Mr. Hume, that miracles are unnatural, not likely to happen; whereas men not speaking the truth is the common experience. You are absolutely right. That is the point about miracles — that they are not likely to happen. If someone rushed in here, as in the old story about St. Thomas Aquinas, crying, "Come to the window, quick, a witch is riding through the sky on a broomstick," which would you say is more likely, that this should really be, or that someone is deluded or deluding us? There is no doubt about which is more likely. But that is not the question. It was not the question for St. Thomas in the story. He dropped the seventy-sixth distinction about something or other in the *Secunda Secundae* and rushed to the window crying, "Where?" And when the brothers laughed, he said, "Better to believe that a witch rides through the air on a broomstick than that a monk should lie."

And that is precisely the kind of an answer Newman gives to Hume:

> Doubtless it is abstractedly more likely that men should lie than that the order of nature should be infringed; but what is abstract reasoning to a question of concrete fact? To arrive at the fact of any matter, we must eschew generalities and take things as they stand, with all their circumstances. *A priori*, of course the acts of men are not so trustworthy as the order of nature, and the pretense of miracles is in fact more common than the occurrence. But

139

the question is not about miracles in general, or men in general, but definitely, whether these particular miracles, ascribed to the particular Peter, James and John are more likely to have been or not.

Not is it more likely that men would lie, but is it more likely that Peter lied, this man, this person, this Peter, whom we know. And for the whole of Christian evidence, beyond Peter, we must finally ask which is more likely, that, for example, there really is life after death or that Jesus lied. We have all memorized this answer long since. It is contained in the Act of Faith: "We believe these truths because Thou hast revealed them Who canst neither deceive nor be deceived." If anyone else revealed them, Hume would be right. But who is being reasonable? Which is more likely? Let us above all be reasonable and choose the likelier course. Which is more likely? That a man could be God or that Jesus — when at His trial He expressly made that claim and went on to suffer and die on the Cross for it — that Jesus told the truth and nothing but the truth? As Chesterton summed the case up in a phrase, a non-Christian has got to believe that Christ — author of the Sermon on the Mount, this man Whom we come to know so well in the course of His history in the New Testament and in the figures of the Old — that this man was at the same time either a liar or a lunatic. Now let us appeal to experience, as Hume would have us do. What is our experience of liars and lunatics? Do they speak sermons on the mount? There are men who claim to be God — they are for the most part in asylums. Are they anything like Him? And if, on the basis of a totally irrational prejudice that no miracle can possibly be true despite your experience, you pick the New Testament apart, ascribing this to truth and that to someone else's lies or lunacy, you will discover in the end that the more you tear it down the more it will cohere and that the Christ of the trial is the same as the Christ of the sermons, that the Christ of the beautiful maxims cannot be torn from the Christ of the miracles, and that the maxims you cannot deny as being beautiful and good and sane are of a piece with the harsher maledictions that repel you because to avoid them you would have to change your life. You cannot evade Newman's case by higher criticism. The Apostles, though they knew Him directly and personally, had a time as hard as you believing the ultimate Christian fact, and with them, and with Doubting Thomas touching His wounds, you have to say, like the consequences or not, "My Lord and my God."

One other example will illustrate both the method and the proof and at the same time afford some glimpse of the depth of Newman's vision beyond mere controversy against an even more famous assault on Christianity:

> An argument has been often put forward by unbelievers
> to this effect that [and Newman quotes Thomas Paine]:
> "A revelation which is to be received as true, ought to be
> written on the sun."

That fine phrase means that if God went to all the trouble of revelation, he should have plastered it in the most obvious place in the universe for all to see, so that none could possibly miss it any more than he would miss the sun. All right, let us retort. If God reveals, surely He will reveal in such a way that no man of good will could doubt. He will not hide His light under a bushel. If Christianity is true, it will be obviously true for all men to see — if they look. And what is the reply? Written on the sun? But it is! Christ is the light of the world.

> Till these last centuries, the Visible Church was, at least
> to her children, the light of the world, as conspicuous as
> the sun in the heavens; and the Creed was written on her
> forehead, and proclaimed through her voice, by a teaching
> as precise as it was emphatical; in accordance with the
> text, "Who is she that looketh forth at the dawn, fair as the
> moon, bright as the sun, terrible as an army set in array?"

Newman admits in this same magnificent passage that Paine has a *prima facie* case against us; at least in the course of her history the Church has suffered some embarrassing eclipses. What about the Borgia popes, Tetzel, and all the rest? What about this argument for the person of the Church in history, this visible body of Christ? We must agree that the Church cannot be defended lightly. But take it all in all from Adam until now. The Church, first in figure in the history of the Jews and then in fact, has been the light of the world; and without the Church, broken as she is, the darkness would be unbearable. For those who border on despair, especially now, it is essential to remember that the Church has never looked so much like Christ as when she was broken and betrayed from within.

Newman began his *Essay on the Development of Christian Doctrine* trying to find a *via media* between the extreme factions of Catholicism and Protestantism. He began to examine, stage by stage, the actual life history of Christendom in order to prove just where and when and under what circumstances the original primitive Church had gone wrong. He concluded that "to be deep in history is to cease to be a Protestant." Newman did not argue this proposition; he discovered it against his own best will. He had retorted upon himself to conclude that there was no real reason why an Anglican should not be a Catholic. The *Essay on the Development of Christian Doctrine* is the book of a man "turning around" not so much to discover where he ought to go as to see where he was. Its very last words are Simeon's:

> *Nunc dimittis servum tuum, Domine,*
> *Secundum verbum tuum in pace,*
> *Quia viderunt oculi mei salutare tuum.*

These are the words assigned for the last of the Canonical Hours, Compline, taken from the song of Simeon as he sat at the door of the Temple in Jerusalem on the day Our Lord was offered to God, according to the Jewish custom, at the Presentation:

> Now dismiss thy servant, Lord,
> According to thy Word in peace,
> Because my eyes have seen thy salvation . . .

"Written on the sun" — but what if the sun should set? Eighteenth-century indifferentism led to nineteenth-century Liberal toleration, which has led to Modernistic infidelity, to that state so common now in which each of the Ten Commandments is systematically and with malice disobeyed, not out of weakness but by political design. The Law of God is misconstrued as the Rights of Man, God Himself is called an invention and His Name a Tin-Pan-Alley tune, His day a Disneyland. Dishonored parents are consigned to antiseptic bedlams known as rest homes at the first slight cardiac tremor; the termination of unwanted life — murder — is a matter of medical discretion since life is nothing but an accidental sequence of sensations, while fornication and adultery, even unspeakable vice, are "all right so long as those involved have affection for each other." Marriage in fact has become a legal form of prostitution, sworn to for as long as the turning of a screw; and theft indeed is property, legitimated by tax accountants; and truth is managed news.

142

Of the seven deadly sins, sloth, the softly smiling beast, moves its slow thighs out of California. If truth is nothing but opinion, right springs from the barrel of a gun. Liberalism is the smiling face of Modernism. Behind it lies the grinning skull. As everybody says, we have arrived again at something like the end of ancient Rome, but worse — because after two thousand years of Christianity we are capable of a perverse and theologically exact apostasy no pagan ever knew. Once again the Secular City lies like a snake in the late afternoon sun. Behind the indifference, and the toleration, the desperate shows that mask the death of the soul, the worm coils in the empty sockets of the eyes. He is no myth; that has been the best of his disguises. It was still a crime to do immoral things even thirty years ago, and then the easy, neopagan toleration won. Now again, over a vast and increasing area, it is a crime to be a Christian, and even in the United States, the stain of Antichrist is in the books and taught in schools, deadening the vital centers of cultural life. College campuses, like Germany in the 1920s, stifle in the atmosphere of *The Blue Angel* where Lesbians in black stockings chant the new psychology and intellectually paralyzed professors cry cock-a-doodle-doo to the revolution. And Christians look fearfully toward a second age of martyrdom, this time without the lions, under the reign of a sophisticated terror by lobotomy and drugs to create international, nondenominational, multiracial moral and political imbecility. The Church herself is split by an apostasy within, far worse than any that has ever been without. Christians who have lived in the hope that the Church would save *them* must fight to save the Church. No sooner on the ark than they must man the pumps. Newman stopped the *Nunc dimittis* several lines too short. "Because my eyes have seen thy salvation . . . ." Yes. But any meditation on the Fourth Joyful Mystery of the Presentation that old Simeon sings must take it to the bitter Cross:

> Behold, this child is set for the fall and for the rise of many in Israel, and for a sign that shall be contradicted — yea, and thine own soul a sword shall pierce — that the thoughts of many hearts may be revealed.

To that image of the Church, as the woman clothed with the sun, we must always add the sign of contradiction and the image of the One for Whom the sun went out in the ninth hour, Whom a sword shall pierce.

10 Dark Night
of the Church

On a dark October night, in the teeming rain, an obscure Italian priest arrived at Oxford, having ridden all day long in an outside seat on the London stage. In a warm room at last, not having eaten since dawn, standing before the fire to dry his dripping clothes, suddenly, just before midnight, he received a visitor — one of the most famous men in England and still one of the most famous in the history of English letters, who, acting a bit extravagantly as they did in that romantic age, flung himself at the feet of the startled priest and asked to be received into the Catholic Church.

Years later, in a controversial essay on the nature of Faith, the famous convert wrote:

> The heart is commonly reached, not through reason, but through the imagination, by means of direct impressions, by the testimony of facts and events, by history, by description. Persons influence us, voices melt us, looks subdue us, deeds inflame us. Many a man will live and die upon a dogma; no man will be a martyr for a conclusion.

But if no man will die for a conclusion — for what, then? And does one have to die?

To most men, Newman wrote, argument makes the point in hand only more doubtful, and considerably less impressive. And though he knew and loved it deeply, Newman never thought the Bible was the one thing necessary:

> Bible religion is both the recognized title and the best description of English religion. It consists not in rites or

creeds, but mainly in having the Bible read in Church, in the family and in private. Now I am far from undervaluing that mere knowledge of Scripture which is imparted to the population thus promiscuously . . . it has to a certain point made up for great and grievous losses in its Christianity.

No one ever died for a set of propositions in an argument, he says, or for a set of pictures drawn from the public reading of a book. For what then? And does one have to die? Is the Catholic Faith a crossing into death?

If you had to sum up the whole of the Faith in a single gesture — not in a *Summa Theologica* in three enormous parts, one of which is further subdivided into two, nor even in a catechism of three hundred and seventy questions and their answers for a penny — but in a single gesture distinguishing the Catholic at once, it is the sign of the Cross: in a single gesture, all of what theologians call the principal mysteries. Press two fingers on the thumb — three persons in one nature of God; fold the other two fingers back into the palm — two natures in one Person of Christ; then trace upon yourself, in the Name of the Father and of the Son and of the Holy Ghost, Christ's sacrifice, which is the Sacrament of the Catholic Altar. It is a dangerous thing to make that sign because it says: I commit myself to that death. Catholics do not trace the descent of the Dove upon themselves, or the star of Hope, or any other sign. As St. Paul said,

> God forbid that I should glory, save in the cross of our
> Lord Jesus Christ; by whom the world is crucified to me,
> and I to the world.

And then he adds these mysterious words to which not very much attention is paid except by saints — by St. Francis of Assisi, for example — who understood them:

> From henceforth let no man be troublesome to me; *for I*
> *bear the marks of the Lord Jesus in my body.*

St. Paul, though not a famous Jewish man of letters, is certainly the most famous Jewish convert. By what was he convinced? As a

Pharisee he knew the Scriptures by heart; it was not Scripture that convinced him. There is no evidence that he had argued with anyone before his sudden change on the road to Damascus — which was a miracle, you say. But had no one — nothing — disposed him to receive the grace? Every conversion is a miracle, yet apologetics arms us against the sin of presumption, the sin that says, "Let's leave it all to God." Apologetics is an effort to dispose — granted that God is the author of such efforts too. But who or what disposed St. Paul to grace? What were the human instruments of his conversion — or of Newman's?

Since Faith is the evidence of things unseen, there really is no case for what rationalist Protestants and Deists of the eighteenth century called "Christian evidence." God left no fingerprints, no secret files to be disclosed, no tapes to play. It is true that St. Paul said the visible things of the world lead to the invisible things of God, but the way is negative and indirect. We cannot prove the Faith from nature but rather — since nature and faith can never contradict — we refute attempts to *disprove* faith from nature. The only direct apologetics of the Catholic Church have been (1) the testimony of witnesses, (2) the experience of persons who lived the Faith, chiefly under monastic rule, and saw for themselves — though in a glass darkly — that it is true, and (3) arguments deriving from the testimony of witnesses and from personal experience — that is, from the first two ways. All these three are really aspects of one apologetic expressed by different emphases, with all three always necessary in the general sense, though not for each person.

Liberal theologians, basing their contentions on an evolutionary view of doctrine, have imagined there are three distinct stages in the history of the Church, the second following on the destruction of the first, and the third on the destruction of the second, like a three-stage rocket. In fact, however, the three are integral: all of them always, everywhere present. It is true that for the first three hundred years the chief defense was that of witnesses — the Greek word for which is "martyr." By dying for the Faith they gave testimony to its validity. But the *Apology* of St. Justin, and catechetical texts such as the *Didache*, attest to the presence of arguments right from the start; and from the Apocalypse, St. Dionysius, and the Desert Fathers we can see that right from the start the testimony of martyrs and teaching of creeds was confessed in the dark, silent night of individual souls.

146

From the conversion of Constantine, when the new religion was made safe for Roman citizens, there was a brief, both terrible and glorious, flaming out of argument in the Arian and Pelagian controversies and the defense of Saints Athanasius, Hilary, Augustine, Jerome, and others, defined in the great Councils, though it did not last long enough to constitute an age — within a lifetime the safety of the Empire had collapsed under the barbarian invasions. St. Augustine wrote the last pages of the *City of God* while his diocesan city was under siege by the Vandals, who sacked it within weeks of his death. Throughout the next thousand years, which is the second age of the Church, the deaths of martyrs continued, and the creeds and controversial works of the Fathers were patiently copied out in monastic scriptoria — but in those great Dark Ages of the Church, as one who knows dark nights would expect, the chief apologetic was the life of countless silent monks and nuns living the Benedictine rule.

Monasticism is essentially the schooling of the personal experience of the Catholic Faith. To believe, one must taste and see. But to do that correctly, he must submit to a rigorous mortification of body and soul to purify and cleanse the windows of perception and intelligence. Otherwise how can the sunlight get through? "Vacate et videte," David said. "Be empty of all things and see that I am God." Those who seek God by themselves in an undisciplined private monasticism "live in their own sheepfold and not the Lord's," says St. Benedict. In the thirteenth century, once again, the arguments flashed out, against the Moslem and Albigensian theologians. The works of Saints Albert, Thomas, Bonaventure and the rest of the Schoolmen of the third great age — the Scholastic age — of the Church fueled a roaring furnace of doctrine, glazing with their heat at last the complete and formal jar of Trent. Since then the Church has been poured out like a libation on a dying world.

Where are we now? Some think this is the dawning of the age of a Catholic Aquarius, of a new emerging Church, whose God is change. I think, like Dante, that in the middle of the journey of our life we have awakened in a dark wood to find the straight way lost. There is a certain truth in every error — which does not make the error true; but to refute an error properly you must not merely show it to be false. That never gets to the heart of it. Like the devils it comes back a hundredfold unless you liberate the truth in it that sets it free. The Modernist war against the Church in our time has often taken the form of an attack on creeds and dogmas. Modernists have accused the Church of Phariseeism — of sticking to the letter that kills against the spirit that gives life. Often they cite Newman, who said no one ever died for a conclusion — forgetting that in the very same sentence he distinguished conclusions from dogmas, expressly saying that indeed men will "live and die upon a dogma," which is a fixed, infallible, irreformable, absolutely unchangeable, exact formulation of belief. If you kill the letter, you will not have the spirit of the letter; and if you try to have a Church of the Holy Spirit without Christ, His commandments, and His formulas in dogmatic definitions, you will not have a Church of the Holy Spirit, because the Holy Spirit is the Spirit of Christ.

Nonetheless, it is true that the letter killeth and the spirit giveth life. It is true that even if a child memorizes the questions and answers of a catechism, he will not be fully educated in the Faith. It does not follow, however, that if he does not memorize the catechism, he will be educated in the Faith. The Creed is not enough, but faith and the dogmas that articulate faith are absolutely necessary, without which there can be no love of God.

In the contemplative life the martyr and the schoolman are welded to each other in the living flame of love. With all due respect to generations who kept the catechisms and creeds in the teeth of violent opposition and cold indifference, and to those who are fighting today to keep them in the face of an indescribable silliness, it is true that the spiritual life of the Church has sometimes tended to dry up in favor of the recitation of formulas and even the raising of money and the administration of an immense physical plant. The response of some has been to deny the truth of the formulas, to tear out altars and burn the images of Mary and the saints, when what is needed is the leaven of St. Benedict — that a significant number of the Church would sacrifice themselves to God as monks and nuns; and that a greater number among priests and laymen would participate in that sacrifice by nourishing the interior life insofar as that is possible in the midst of their active duties in the world.

The Catholic Church has a rich deposit of faith and a fecund life even today germinating in its soil — martyrs, monks, and theologians, all calling with the same quiet voice, not seeking publicity, calling softly but insistently from the Gulag Archipelago and the desert cells, from isolated schools, and even from the silent hearts of nameless persons in the lonely crowds who kneel before the Blessed

Sacrament — if they can find it — or stop to pray in empty churches and in quiet rooms. The arguments of scholastic theology codified at Trent, capsulated in catechism texts, amplified by the ordinary and extraordinary magisterium of the Church these last four hundred years — all this is based upon and animated by the experience of the spiritual life of the contemplative monk and nun and of the soldiers of the militant orders leading what St. Thomas calls the mixed life, and even of laymen like St. Thomas More who, though chancellor of England, led a hidden life, wore a hair shirt beneath his public silks, and ended up a martyr to the Faith as well. In turn, the hidden life of contemplatives seeks its consummation in death transfigured by love. It is no accident that the greatest doctor of the spiritual life is named St. John of *the Cross*.

The scholastic arguments from revelation and reason begin and end in the sign of the Cross. The spiritual experience learned in the monastic life according to the twelve steps of humility in the rule of St. Benedict, commented on by St. Bernard and expanded by St. John of the Cross, is the total sacrifice of the five exterior senses and of the three interior faculties of intellect, memory, and will. Its consummation is the Spiritual Marriage in which one dies of love.

> Oh, living flame of love
> That tenderly woundest my
> Soul in its deepest center,
> Since thou art no longer oppressive, perfect me
> Now if it be thy will. Break the web of this
> Sweet encounter. [13]

St. John of the Cross explains the meaning of his own verses:

> Perfect me now if it be thy will. . . . That is to say: Perfect and consummate the spiritual marriage in me with the beatific vision of Thyself — for it is this that the soul breathes. . . . This desire will never be satisfied or at rest until its glory shall appear [in death] especially if it has already tasted the sweetness and delight thereof, which it

---

[13]Quotations are all from Allison Peers' translation of *The Complete Works of St. John of the Cross*, Garden City, N.Y., 1962.

has in this state. This sweetness is such that, had God not granted a favour to its flesh, and covered its natural being with His right hand (as He did to Moses in the rock, that he might see His glory and not die) it would have died at each touch of this flame, and its natural being would have been destroyed, since its lower part would have no means of enduring so great and sublime a fire of glory. Therefore it must be known, with regard to the natural dying of souls that reach this state, that, though the manner of their death, from the natural standpoint, is similar to that of others, yet in the cause and mode of their death there is a great difference. For while the deaths of others may be caused by infirmities or length of days, when these souls die, although it may be from some infirmity, or from old age, their spirits are wrested away by nothing less than some loving impulse and encounter. . . . For this reason David said that the death of saints in the fear of God was precious, for at such a time all the riches of the soul come to unite together, and the rivers of love of the soul are about to enter the sea, and these are so broad and dense and motionless that they seem to be seas already.

St. Alphonsus Liguouri says:

Mary, by a singular privilege granted to no other saint, loved, and was always actually loving God in every moment of her life, with such ardor, that St. Bernard declares, it required a continued miracle to preserve her life in the midst of such flames. . . . As the loving Virgin lived, so did she die. As divine love gave her life, so did it cause her death; for the Doctors and Holy Fathers of the Church generally say she died of no other infirmity than pure love. St. Francis de Sales says the Blessed Virgin's life was a perpetual act of contemplation. Therefore at length the sacred fire of this divine love consumed her entirely as a sweet holocaust, so that she died in that fire, her soul being wholly swept up and transported into the arms of her Son's most special love. O death, living by love, O love, dying of life!

150

Mark you, I have quoted only Doctors of the Church — in this reckless age, if you read spiritual books at all, read none but those of saints, no matter how good anyone else may be. In the limited time you have, read the saints. They are simpler than you might think and they know what they are talking about. And if you meditate on the Fourth Glorious Mystery of the Rosary, remember that the Assumption, which was Mary's death, was precisely the touch of this flame that is the whole reason for the Catholic life. Each of us, despite our weaknesses and worse, must in some final hour "break the web of that sweet encounter." And to do that we must, as Mary did, go through a narrow gate and walk on a narrow way. St. Francis de Sales says:

> Various sacred lovers were present at the death of the Savior. Among them, those having the greatest sorrow, for love was then deeply plunged into sorrow and sorrow into love. All those who were filled with loving passion for their Savior were in love with His passion and sorrow. But His sweet Mother, who loved Him more than all others, was more than all others pierced through and through by the sword of sorrow. Her Son's sorrow at that time was a piercing sword that passed through the Mother's heart, for that Mother's heart was fastened, joined, and united to her Son in so perfect a union that nothing could wound the one without inflicting the keenest torture upon the other. . . . Mary not only sought no cure for its wound, but loved that wound more than any cure and dearly guarded the shafts of sorrow she had received because of the love that had sped them into her heart. Continually she desired to die for them, since her Son died of them. For as all the Holy Scriptures and all the learned say, He died amid the flames of charity, a perfect holocaust for all the sins of the world.[14]

And St. John of the Cross says that there is no way to be kindled in that flame of love except through the wood of the Cross. For us who, unlike Mary, have been touched by sin, that Cross we bear is not only His but our own.

---

[14]*On the Love of God*, trans. with notes by John K. Ryan, Garden City, N.Y., 1963.

On a dark night,
Kindled in love with yearnings —
Oh, happy chance! — I went forth without being
Observed, my house being now at rest.

This night, St. John of the Cross says, is an

inflowing of God into the soul . . . which is called by
contemplatives infused contemplation, or Mystical
Theology. Herein God secretly teaches the soul and in-
structs it in perfection and love. . . . But the question
arises: Why is the Divine Light . . . here called . . . a dark
night? . . . Because the light and wisdom of this contemplation is most bright and pure, and the soul which it
assails is dark and impure, it follows that the soul suffers
great pain when it receives it in itself, just as when the eyes
are dimmed by humors and become impure and weak, the
assault made upon them by a bright light causes them
pain. And when the soul suffers the direct assault of this
Divine Light, its pain, which results from its impurity, is
immense; because, when this pure light assails the soul, in
order to expel its impurity, the soul feels itself to be so
impure and miserable that it believes God to be against it,
and thinks that it has set itself up against God. This causes
it sore grief and pain, because it now believes that God has
cast it away: this was one of the greatest trials which Job
felt when God sent him this experience, and he said,
"Why hast Thou set me contrary to Thee, so that I am
grievous and burdensome to myself? Have pity upon me,
have pity upon me, at least ye, my friends, because the
hand of the Lord has touched me."

I wonder how many, thrilled by the sentimental song from
Superstar, "He Touched Me," have ever read the Book of Job and
thought what that hour will be like when it really happens to them.
St. John of the Cross recalls the prophet Jeremiah's description of the
touch of the hand of God:

I am the man that sees my poverty in the rod of His
indignation; he hath threatened me and brought me into

darkness and not into light. So far hath He turned against me and hath converted His hand upon me all the day! My skin and my flesh hath He made old; He hath broken my bones; He hath made a fence around me and compassed me with gall and trial; He hath set me in dark places, as those that are dead forever. He hath made a fence around me and against me, that I may not go out; He hath made my captivity heavy. Yea, and when I have cried and have entreated, He hath shut out my prayer. He hath enclosed my paths and ways out with square stones; He hath thwarted my steps. He hath set ambushes for me; He hath become to me a lion in a secret place. He hath turned aside my steps and broken me in pieces. He hath made me desolate; He hath bent His bow and set me as a mark for His arrow. He hath shot into my reins the draughts of His quiver. I have become a derision to all people, and laughter and scorn for them all the day. He hath filled me with bitterness and hath made me drunken with wormwood. He hath broken my teeth by number, He hath fed me with ashes. My soul is cast out from peace; I have forgotten good things. And I said: Mine end is frustrated and cut short, together with my desire and my hope from the Lord. Remember my poverty and my excess, the wormwood and the gall. I shall be mindful with remembrance and my soul shall be undone within my pains.

If you desire the conversion of America; if you believe in the right to life and have worked for constitutional changes to protect unborn children, or if you love the poor, the persecuted, and the sick — if, in a word, you are generous, Christ says you must not just give something of yourself but everything. The Doctors of the Catholic Church teach very clear doctrine to generous souls: You cannot give what you have not got. You cannot make another be what you are not or do what you do not do. You cannot ignite the wood unless you are a flame. Fire makes fire. And there is only one way to be a Christian. Christ said, "I am the way." And His way is the way of the Cross — which leads, as in His dying words He said, to a consummation in the death of love. *Consummatum est.* It is consummated. The work is done — the work of doing the will of the Father, which is to unite our hearts to His, reserving nothing — and of all the saints who ever loved Our Lord, the one who died most perfectly died, as St. Alphonsus and all the Fathers and Doctors say, of love.

This is what Newman meant when he said that no one ever died for a conclusion. He did not repudiate the Church of creeds. The creed of St. Athanasius was his favorite prayer. What he meant was that a creed is not only a set of propositions presented to the intellect — which it is — but more, it is a prayer, grounded in the blood of Christ and the martyrs, and confirmed in the spiritual fire of the love and death of Mary and all virgins and confessors.

Who or what, then, predisposed St. Paul to his conversion? We know the answer from the Book of Acts:

> And casting him forth without the city, they stoned him; and the witnesses laid down their garments at the feet of a young man whose name was Saul. And they stoned Stephen, invoking, and saying, Lord Jesus receive my spirit. And falling on his knees, he cried out with a loud voice, saying: Lord, lay not this sin to their charge. And when he had said this, he fell asleep in the Lord. And Saul was consenting to his death.

St. Stephen — the first martyr — must have seen him; perhaps their eyes met an instant and Stephen winked in that intersection of eternity and time: St. Stephen proto-martyr and the young, intolerant man whose name was Saul.

And who or what had prepared Newman for that dark October night in the teeming rain in 1845? Almost forty years before, in 1808, Napoleon had invaded Rome. In 1809 he called up Italian conscripts as cannon fodder for his vast campaigns, ending in the bitter Russian cold. Of forty thousand young men drafted from the Papal States, two thousand returned home. A seventeen-year-old youth, not about to serve a detested, sacrilegious emperor and not about to die — a young man, exceptional in the intensity of his prayers, but otherwise an adolescent like the others, struck a bargain with God. Years later he retold the story in an autobiographical sketch:[15]

---

[15]See Alfred Wilson, *Blessed Dominic Barberi*, London, 1967.

On the night before the lots were drawn, I knelt down as usual to make my meditation on the Passion of Christ [which he had learned a short time before on a retreat conducted by the Passionist Fathers]. Towards the end, I felt inspired to make a conditional vow that if I escaped conscription, and if religious orders were re-established [in Italy after Napoleon's interdiction] I would become a Passionist. Sensitively alive as I was to my extreme frailty, especially in the matter of chastity, I placed myself under the special protection of my great patron St. John the Evangelist, and then pronounced my vow in the following words: Lord, here in Your Presence, and in the presence of Most Holy Mary, my Guardian Angel, and St. John the Evangelist, I promise and vow that if You exempt me from the hazards of military service and re-establish Religious Orders, I will become a Passionist. Mary Most Holy, be my protectress and advocate; I place my vow in your hands. Angel Guardian, be a witness of my offering; and you, Holy Apostle, accept the task of keeping me firm in my resolution to preserve chastity. I place myself in your hands. It is up to you to present me, pure and undefiled, to the Divine Judge. I commit the care of myself entirely to you. You are well aware of my extreme fraility and that I am good for nothing but sin, so you must look after me!

A childish vow, no doubt, in childish phraseology. But when the lot was drawn, he was exempt. "After such manifest divine protection," he wrote in the autobiography,

one would naturally expect that I dedicated myself with renewed fervor to the divine service. What else could one expect? Since benefits bind the heart, these benefits ought to have bound my heart most securely. But heart I had none. Wretch that I am, mine must be a heart of bronze, not flesh. For God and the wretched men who had been dragged off to the war, I scarce spared a thought, least of all was I concerned about one particular young man who had shown interest in a girl I fancied.

Yet, ten years later, by a series of intricate accidents out of which life seems to be constructed, he was ordained a Passionist. It was as if an invisible string were drawing in his soul. He writes about his doubts and fears, praying to Mary a few days after his ordination:

O mother mine, my confusion is so great that I can hardly stand. I implore you to help me never to abuse this dignity of the priesthood. The very thought of that possibility makes me shudder with horror. Sometimes, as I am walking to the altar, I am forced to stop to reassure myself that I really am a priest. I can hardly believe it. What! I say to myself, a few years ago I was — God knows! And now I have to celebrate Holy Mass, and, at the thought of it, I feel the blood freeze in my veins . . . Virgin Most Holy, you understand. There is no need to tell you. As I handled the Sacred Host, how can I describe what I experienced? You alone could describe it who handled that Divine Body so worthily. But as for me, how do I treat it? Ah, my Heavenly Mother, that is what horrifies me. How different would it be if I had your purity, your sanctity. When I am about to celebrate, how I long to have your heart as fitting resting place for my Jesus; your hands with which to touch Him; and your voice, to summon Him to the holy altar. But I have neither your voice, nor your hands, nor your heart. Far from it, I am a mass of iniquity, and I tremble at the thought. And yet, Jesus my Lord and my God is so kind! He allows me to deal with Him as He did the cruel executioners who nailed Him to the cross. I say to Him: My Jesus, behold in me Judas, Your executioner. Your crucifier. And yet He is not offended by all this. He takes pleasure, it almost seems, in being treated like this by me, a miserable wretch. Instead of reproving me for my temerity in approaching Him, He even appears to invite me, and is wishful to enter my unworthy heart.

A year later, on February 21, 1819, by a still more inexplicable impulse, he struck another bargain with God. (February 21st, incidentally, is Cardinal Newman's birthday.) This is from the young Italian priest's diary at that time. He was twenty-seven years old.

This morning I experienced intense feelings of love of Jesus and realized how absolutely one ought to be entirely His. I burned with desire to make all love Him, no matter what trials the attempt to do so might cost me. Since I am always safe when hidden in Him, I will strive never to be parted from Him, and whenever His glory is at stake, even if I have to sacrifice my life a thousand times over, I will not flinch . . . My Jesus! Would that I could annihilate myself, if by so doing, I could contribute even a little to your glory; would that my voice could make itself heard to the ends of the earth crying to all, Love Jesus Christ, Love Jesus Christ . . . . I will simply keep in the Divine Presence, and make neither reflections nor requests. In this way, I shall unite my heart to God, and desire only what God desires, which will not be little.

"Not be little" indeed — because God took him at his word. Looking back sixteen years later, he vividly describes this moment of his sacrifice:

My God, what agony I experienced then. My soul seemed to be torn from my body, no it was more than that. I think that if my soul had been torn from my body, I should not have experienced such pain. It was rather as if the soul was torn from the soul; even that does not describe it, it was more, more . . . . I experienced a pain so lively, so penetrating, so fierce, such as I have never experienced before. I believe that only the sorrow of the damned in hell can exceed that pain . . . I seemed to swoon . . . I know not how I lived through it.

His favorite text at this time became: "Unless the grain of wheat die, itself remaineth alone." But seven months later, in October, he renewed his vow and took upon himself another extraordinary and mysterious burden — nothing less than the conversion of England. "In this month of October," he wrote in his diary,

I have experienced a great longing for the conversion of unbelievers, especially of England, and I have offered

157

myself to God to be annihilated, if annihilation could serve this purpose. I must make sure that this desire is never extinguished, for I am certain that, if I persevere, God will be moved to pity. I intend now, in the presence of God, to ratify all my former promises. Lord, if you wish me to go mad, or to be unfrocked or hung, or ostracized from human society; if You wish to annul me; if You wish to condemn me to Purgatory until the day of Judgment; if You wish to deprive me of Your sensible help, if You wish that I should never enjoy any satisfaction in prayer, or that I should be tormented by scruples; if You wish to condemn me to suffer all the pains that the English would have to suffer if they were damned, I am content, provided only that they all return to You. My God, I protest that I will never allow my heart any consolation until I witness their conversion. If You desire to give me a proof of Your love, open the way to their conversion, in whatever way pleases you. I do not ask this through any merits of my own, but through the merits of the Precious Blood shed by Your Divine Son, through the merits of Mary Most Holy, and through the intercession of all the saints in Heaven. My dear Mother, now it is up to you to obtain this for me. I want it, and all I want is the glory of Your Divine Son and the salvation of my brethren. *Fratres meos quaero.* You are my mother so give me this proof of it; I can enjoy nothing until you do. Don't let this be the first time that I have had a refusal from you. The glory will be yours and your Divine Son's for all eternity. Amen.

Still a sort of childish attitude even at age twenty-seven. On October 5, 1841, twenty-two years later, Father Dominic, now almost fifty years old, was sent to England by his Order in the late fulfillment of a vow he had made so long ago scarcely knowing what he meant. He didn't know much English either — it was a Quixotic choice to preach among the genteel English gentiles. Anti-Catholic feeling was strong enough among the low ones, without this foreign conspirator among them. One day while he was walking through the village where the Passionists had secured a retreat house, a gang of toughs waylaid him. They began to throw stones, one of which struck him in the forehead, opening a gash. He stooped, retrieved the stone — the crowd hesitated — he winked, kissed the stone, and put it into his pocket, walking on.

Of course he is the priest at whose feet, that dark October night of 1845, Newman fell, to be received into the Church.

Some years later, when staying with a group of new converts who came into the Church with Newman, Father Dominic quizzed them about the English language. He wanted to know the worst words to call anybody, he said; he wanted to know the vilest terms of vituperation. Some of the young fellows thought they would play a practical joke on the ridiculous little foreigner. Convinced that he would make a fool of himself arguing with some staid old British dowager, they gave him all the words they knew, which were plenty. Just by chance that night as he was coming to bed, one of the young fellows passed by the open chapel door and heard Father Dominic, kneeling before the Blessed Sacrament, weeping as he struck his chest and in a thick Italian accent said, "O Lord, have mercy on this miserable sonofabitch."

Ten years earlier (long before he had even heard of him), Newman delivered a famous sermon on the theme of Father Dominic's whole life. The text: "Are ye able to drink of the cup that I shall drink of, and to be baptized with the baptism that I am baptized with? And they said, We are able." "If faith be the essence of a Christian life," Newman said, "it follows that our duty lies in risking upon Christ's word what we have, for what we have not."

If anyone should want to convert America, or even his friends or himself, he must risk the death of love. At the present hour we are in a dark night of the Church. The usual ways are lost. There is little comfort in the visible Church now. The liturgy, set upon by thieves, is lying in the ditch; contemplatives are mouthing political slogans in the streets; nuns have lost their habits along with their virtues, virgins their virginity, confessors their consciences, theologians their minds. And, if this is true, it is a "happy chance!" — because there is absolutely no reason left to be Catholic now except the only one there ever really was — that in the invisible life of the Church you will find the love of Christ. But if the Church were lost? That can never be, because, as St. Peter said, there is a soft and gentle candle flame like the vigil light that burns beside the Blessed Sacrament, "a light that shineth in a dark place until the day dawn and the day star arise in your hearts." "Lead, kindly light," Newman had written:

159

Lead, kindly light, amid the encircling gloom,
Lead thou me on.
The night is dark and I am far from home,
Lead thou me on.
Keep thou my feet; I do not ask to see
The distant scene — one step enough for me.

"On a dark night, kindled in love with yearnings — O happy chance!"
said St. John of the Cross.

The greatest need in the Church today is the contemplative life of
monks and nuns. The arguments and public martyrdoms are vain
without the sacrifice of hearts. And what are the argumentas and
sacrifices for, except to bring us to the love of God? Apologetic has the
mind of Thomas and the sword of Paul and the heart of them both and
all the saints including, let us hope, the least of us. The spiritual life is
not just for the great saints; it is the ordinary way of salvation.

Don't be put off by the false humility and inverted snobbery of the
carnal man who sneers at prayer and says it is for mystics, not for
ordinary men. The ordinary man is made for heaven and the only way
to heaven is the Cross, whose straitest gate is a vocation to religious
life where as a monk or nun, formally and under strict rule and
direction, one commits himself entirely, in that burning furnace of
charity, to God's love. There is the active life, but Mary chose the
better part and everything that Martha does depends on her.

There aren't many monasteries left — thank God there are a few,
and a few good books, not difficult to read, though difficult to do.
First, *An Introduction to the Devout Life* by St. Francis de Sales, and
last, his *Treatise on the Love of God;* while in between, the four great
songs of St. John of the Cross, *The Ascent of Mount Carmel, Dark Night
of the Soul, The Spiritual Canticle*, and *The Living Flame of Love;* and the
three of St. Teresa of Avila, the *Autobiography, The Way of Perfection*,
and *The Interior Castle.* [16]

Don't be afraid. Remember James and John who, not knowing
what they meant, said, "We are able." And if you fear your own
incompetence, remember Father Dominic, who kissed the stone —
now officially called Blessed Dominic Barberi on his way to canoniza-
tion, God's poor, miserable sonofabitch.

---

[16] All available in excellent translations in the paperback series of Image Books
published by Doubleday, Garden City, N.Y.

11 Black but Beautiful

When an American cousin asked to view the Roman ruins of Britain, Belloc replied, "Madame, Britain is a Roman ruin." With due respect, I think he should have said a medieval and therefore Christian ruin. If religion is the first determinant of a culture, the declining West is ruined Christendom, about which two positions have been taken — and a third, ignored, suppressed, and not very forcefully put forward.

The first is the Romantic love of the ruins themselves. As Herodotus said, give the dead their meed of praise. The Romantic sheds an idle tear for battles long ago, and ah, the days that are no more.

> Miniver sighed for what was not
> And dreamed, and rested from his labors;
> He dreamed of Thebes and Camelot,
> And Priam's neighbors.

According to the second view, which was Thucydides', the business of history, like that of the law court, is to get the facts, establish precedents, and offer future generations arguments in similar cases. Gibbon was the first Thucydides of Christendom, seeing it as the vast Sicilian campaign of a misguided Rome. He tried to prove that Nero, after all, was right about who set Rome afire; it was the Christians, finally, who did the Romans in and not, as St. Augustine said, themselves and their lying gods. Just as Thucydides had placed the Nature Philosophers and the Sophists at his service, so the modern scientific historian has applied the methods of Newton to the case — in this case, Christendom — and the first wave was a demolition, beginning with Gibbon, rising to a fury in the nineteenth century.

161

Andrew D. White, first chancellor of Cornell University, for example, wrote the multivolume history of a dispute he called *The Warfare of Science and Theology*. White collected the best library of medieval material in America for the purpose of exposing what he called the Christian superstition. A Gothic chapel was built on campus with stained-glass windows illustrating — instead of legends of the saints — great moments in science like Ben Franklin flying his kite.

> O ghastly glories of saints, dead limbs of gibbeted gods,
> Though all men abase them before, in spirit — and all knees bend,
> I kneel not, neither adore you, but standing look to the end!

Lynn Thorndike at Columbia wrote an encyclopedia of what he called medieval magic as the superstitious matrix of modern science, and Henry Dana Lea at Johns Hopkins rivaled White of Cornell with his collections and indictments. In England, G. G. Coulton made a caricature of the position, climaxed in the hilarious debate with Chesterton, who summed it up in the famous quip: "I never met a man who knew so much and understood so little."

In the last half century a more sober, if duller, view of scientific medieval studies has prevailed, whose purpose is not so much to exterminate Christianity as to understand its effects — provided they are measurable. The longbow, stirrup, and the moldboard plow, the catalogue of manuscripts at Fulda — hard evidence, not the evidence of things unseen; the accomplishments of St. Thomas in philosophy, not the *Tantum ergo* or his vision of the Cross. Six thousand years of evidence, according to the Biblical number, is ignored — I mean the evidence of an interior life.

For example, Henry Osborne Taylor thinks of himself as praising St. Augustine and promoting more sympathetic attitudes in medieval studies when he says:

> In matters of sheer intellect Augustine rises creative above his contemporaries. He anticipates Descartes' *Cogito ergo sum* and almost Kant's thought of the subjectivity of time.

One can hear the devil from the Book of Acts replying, "I know who Augustine is, but who are Descartes and Kant?" St. Augustine is the Plato of Christendom. All theology is a footnote to St. Augustine. He is certainly not the pilot fish of a French geometer or a German pedant. "Despite his great intellect," Dr. Taylor goes on, "he had some of the limitations of his time. He believed in miracles." Are miracles the limitations of one's time? In a sense St. Augustine said indeed they are — limits of all times, limits of time itself. *Hodiernus tuus, aeternitas.* Augustine laughed at the village atheists of his day who could not believe the water really changed to wine at Cana when it happens every year in the slower miracle of the vintage where the gentle rain is taken up in a kind of transubstantiation by the grapes.

Likewise, Taylor says,

> he assumes the existence of angels and reasons on their creation and on their knowledge of God . . . He had also the universal habit of allegorical interpretations, with fancies for the symbolism of numbers.

Did St. Paul suffer from the limitations of his time when he said:

> Tell me, you that desire to be under the law, have you not read the law? . . . in which things are said by an allegory?

Quae sunt per allegoriam dicta? Are angels, too, a fiction of one's time, and is Scripture's own method of interpreting itself a mere fancy? Whose time has limitations?

This first hostile, scientific wave was gravely if uncritically met by the last Romantics of the Gothic Revival, who tempered the fury of science with a marvelous wit that, alas, served only to slow things down — so that a second gentler, sympathetic wave could drown the poor survivors anyhow. Reexamining the data with a prejudice in their favor, the generation of sympathetic scientific historians has even positively asserted a medieval superiority, as in the work of Gilson and Maritain, who argue that St. Augustine, and especially St. Thomas, anticipate all the achievements of the modern world — that is, in a way, you see, they were really modern. Christopher

Dawson, who tried to prove that medieval Christianity was responsible for the whole idea of progress, achieved an academic respectability denied to the cantankerous old Romantic, anti-Modern, and greater historian, Belloc. Medieval studies have followed an order of integration into academic respectibility, much as black people have been integrated into white society: at first the minstrel shows and Old Black Joe; then, at the second stage, attempts to prove that blacks are really just like whites, you see them on the television shows, Black Executive, Black Agent 007. Belloc and Chesterton were public entertainers, as they well knew, blackface comedians in a medieval minstrel show; and at the second stage, Neoscholasticism was the philosophic skin of authentic Thomist theology, cosmetically whitened by Liberal politics. But suppose that black itself were beautiful — is the scientific establishment ready to tolerate not just another school of thought, but a profoundly different presence?

Nigra sum sed formosa, filiae Jerusalem.
I am black but beautiful, O daughters of Jerusalem.

After St. Paul's, St. Augustine's is the most celebrated and best documented conversion to Christianity. To understand conversion is to understand what happened in history, and perhaps a great deal more; for the operative causes of conversion are precisely what is studied in the third alternative — in neither Romantic exaggeration nor scientific reduction of the subject, but the experience of it, especially in monastic life, its central institution, devoted to nothing else.

There are four notes in the definition of this kind of learning.

First, the final cause: the purpose of a college, in the medieval view, is not knowledge; or at least not knowledge in the scientific sense, or prudence or art in the ethical and economic senses either — neither a theoretical nor a practical knowledge but what St. Benedict calls *experientia* — meaning an interior experience, not of the senses or of the intelligence working on the data of the senses, but an experience of grace in the gifts of the Holy Spirit, which bring forth the fruits of the Spirit.

St. Augustine at Ostia, with all his university science, was surpassed by his ignorant mother:

The day now approaching that she was to depart this life, which day Thou well knewest, though we were not aware of it, it fell out, Thyself, as I believe, by Thine own secret ways so casting it, that she and I should stand alone, leaning in a certain window, which looked into the garden within the house where we now lay, at Ostia by Tiber . . . [where] by inward musing, and discoursing upon Thee, and by admiring of Thy works . . . we came to our own souls, which we presently went beyond, so that we advanced as high as that religion of never-wasting plenty whence Thou feedest Israel for ever with the food of truth . . . And while we were thus discoursing and panting after it, we arrived to a little touch of it with the whole effort of our heart; and we sighed, and even there we left behind us the first fruits of our spirits enchained to it. *Attingimus eam modice toto ictu cordis.* We touched it just a little by a total stroke of the heart.

St. Monica is like St. Teresa of Avila, constantly protesting her ignorance as the learned Dominicans scrutinize the pages of her autobiography to find a method for their own perfection — a method she knows, as she says a hundred times, not by knowledge but experience.

An ignorant St. Benedict, "knowingly ignorant and wisely untaught," in the famous phrase of St. Gregory the Great, nonetheless calls himself a teacher, a *magister*:

> *Ausculta, o fili, praecepta magistri, et inclina aurem cordis tui.*
> Hearken, my son, to the precepts of the teacher and incline the ear of thy heart.

The ear of the heart, not the brain — and that is the difference. St. Augustine had said at Ostia — *ore cordis,* "we panted with the mouth of our heart after those upper streams of thy fountains." St. Benedict's rule is called the constitution of a school, but not for the sake of mere knowledge:

Constituenda est ergo nobis dominici schola servitii.
We must establish a school of the Lord's service —

in whose curriculum the student grows in "conversation" —

processu vero conversationis.

Abbot McCann translates the much commented word simply as "monastic life," meaning not only talk, but every thought and gesture, not by an inflation of the mind but a dilation of the heart, the student runs with an unutterable sweetness, like St. John outrunning Peter at Mary Magdalen's news about the empty tomb. *Dulcis* — sweet — is a Benedictine word, especially St. Bernard's, the Mellifluous Doctor, who is said to have composed one of the perfect poems of the mystical tradition from David to St. John of the Cross.

> *Jesu dulcis memoria*
> *dans vera cordis gaudia,*
> *sed super mel et omnia,*
> *ejus dulcis presentia.*

> Jesus, the very thought of thee
> With sweetness fills the breast,
> But sweeter far thy face to see
> And in thy presence rest.

Even Newman in *The Idea of a University* takes it for granted that the aim of education is knowledge. His quarrel is first to insist on the inclusion of theology as the branch and crown of it, and second to distinguish teaching from research. Philosophers of education generally agree, disputing means not ends. It has been rather the social scientists and psychologists who have rediscovered the monastic principle of learning as experience — though, ignorant of Plato, they have taken totalitarian socialization as the only alternative to the intellectual tradition.

Abbot McCann, in his fine edition of St. Benedict's *Rule*, takes his epigraph — surprisingly at first — not from a Christian source:

> For it is no ordinary matter that we are discussing but the right conduct of life.

The word in Greek is *tropos*, the "turning" of life, exactly as in *conversio* and *conversatio*, whose root is *vertere*, "to turn." The quotation is from Socrates speaking to Thrasymachus in the *Republic* — and one could cite the whole of *Symposium*, *Phaedrus*, and *Phaedo*, indeed his collected works, to prove that Plato, like St. Benedict, thinks the end of education is the love of wisdom — *philosophia* — not the acquisition of facts and skills; the difference, of course, is in Who that wisdom is. As St. Augustine said of the Platonists, "The Word made flesh, that found I not among them."

The second note of a monastic education is its formal cause, the way, the *via* or *cursus* on which the eager student runs, which is, as Socrates said, "the entire conduct of life," not so many credit-hours of more or less related subjects. The chief formal criticism of the modern university from this point of view is its failure in integrity — studies are not integral, there is no integer, they are not one. It is not a university but a pluriversity, whose cultural life is largely left to the entertainment industry, and even within the academic program there is little relation made among technical specialties.

St. Benedict, like Socrates in the *Symposium*, says the curriculum is a ladder of love, whose sides are the body and the soul, with twelve rungs of humility leading from earth to heaven like the ladder in the dream of Jacob with descending and ascending angels, God Himself leaning over the top with a mild surmise. For the training of the body there is the ascetic life — the habit, the fare, the manual work; and for the soul, the liturgy, the *Opus Dei* as St. Benedict called it, the continuous total immersion in a very few texts — the Psalter learned by heart in the first year of the novitiate and finally the whole of the Old and New Testaments in St. Jerome's vulgar Latin. Beside the Bible were the *Rule* and a few select commentaries. No single monastery ever had anything like the bulk of the *Patrologia*. The monks read very little of their own tradition and still less of the liberal arts.

Attempts to prove eighth-, twelfth-, and thirteenth-century Renaissances are tendentious, and assume, of course, a modern theory of progress. Few in those days read the Greeks at all or even any classical Latin other than some schoolboy books for learning grammar. As soon as Plato was taken up in St. Augustine, there was no longer any need for Plato. As the children of Israel took vessels of Egyptian gold and silver with them in the wilderness, so Christendom took some of this and that — but not very much. As with Buddha's raft across the Ganges, it would be absurd, once having used the classics to get to St.

167

Augustine, to strap them on one's back and continue studying Virgil and Cicero on the dry land of Christendom. Old G. G. Coulton was right, I think: they were a narrow, antiliberal lot, if you measure them by the world's standards. Even the most learned of them, such as Alcuin, was no Socrates or even a Flaccus, as they jokingly called him; and when you consider the millions of monks in all the monasteries across the Dark Ages for a thousand years from the bitter western isles of Britain to the deserts of Egypt, those ages really were dark. If Plato was right in his famous analogy, and history is the progress of the soul writ large, these ages were the Dark Night of Christendom of which St. John of the Cross might have written:

> Oh, night more lovely than the dawn,
> Oh, night that joined Beloved with lover,
> Lover transformed in the Beloved.
> On my flowery breast, kept wholly for himself alone,
> There he stayed sleeping, and I caressed him,
> And the fanning of the cedars made a breeze.

Narrow the way and strait the gate into this garden. I spent some part of a long winter a few paces away from the ruins of St. Colman's Abbey on Inishbofin off the west coast of Ireland. In the cloister there it was like walking on a rough sea because the bones of all those ancient monks heave from their graves in many a mouldering heap. And such a little place, on a narrow island. But the view through the east window of the chapel over what was once the altar is as wide, I think, as anyone has ever seen. In what sense is the mind narrow that has not so much studied as become the substance of the Psalms? Day after day, hour upon hour, summer, winter, through the watches of the night, humming with a resonating sound that buzzes in the skull and bones, the long, slow-balanced verses and antiphons in the singular, sonorous silence of the Gregorian tones. We have confused simplicity with impoverishment and poverty with destitution. What sort of culture was this and what sort of man was formed in it? One thinks of Newman's ideal of the nineteenth-century gentleman, weaned on Cicero, finished in the liberal sciences and arts to flourish earnestly in the Foreign Service; or of the eighteenth-century Londoner, full of wit and vulgar vigor; or of the Renaissance polymath, brilliant, lewd, skeptical, and sly, schooled in the Abbey of Thélème and the workshops of Cellini and the Prince. Look on these several portraits — which is Hyperion, which the Satyr? Romanesque and Gothic, both are accidental accomplishments of the cloister, spin-offs of a life of prayer. Suger was Abbot of St. Denys, his spiritual director St. Bernard, whose hymns and sermons, especially on the Song of Songs — who shall measure them? The same Dante who took Virgil as his guide through hell and purgatory, placed St. Bernard next to the Blessed Virgin over all the other stars in the heaven of heavens of the *Paradiso* and composed perhaps the finest lyric in the Italian language — in imitation of him — for him to sing. Just to glance at these pictures quickly is enough to prove at least that no one can exclude a culture such as this on the grounds that it was ignorant and narrow — which it was!

Read aloud, as the monks do, in *lectio divinis*, in a low tone to yourself or among a few friends, Sermon XXVI, whose text is the Song of Songs 1: 4:

> *Sicut tabernacula Cedar, sicut pelles Salomonis.*
> As the tents of Kedar, as the curtains of Solomon.

St. Bernard comments carefully, according to the tradition, using Scripture to interpret Scripture, himself a living concordance — which is not an index but, as the name implies, a knowing by heart. Finding the word *Cedar* in Psalm 119, he quotes the verse:

> Woe is me that sojourning is prolonged . . .

and ruminating on that theme remembers Romans 7:24:

> Unhappy man that I am, who shall deliver me from the body of this death?

and after sixty-six lines of the closely printed text breaks into a heart-rending *quousque*:

> *Quousque enim dissimulo, et ignis quem intra me ipsum abscondo, triste pectus adurit, interiora depascitur?*
> How long shall I dissemble while this fire I hide within me burns my heavy heart and pastures on my entrails?

169

There follows until the end, one of the most intensely personal, objective, and spiritual expressions of grief in the vast literature of death, on the death of his brother Girard —

> *frater sanguine, professione filius, sollicitudine pater, consors spiritu, intimus affectu.*

> brother by blood, by monastic profession son, in solicitude father, consort in spirit, intimate friend in affection.

In recent studies of the Latin language in colleges and universities it is commonly affirmed that programs whose reading does not contain Cicero and Virgil are not just unacceptable but unthinkable. St. Bernard's *quousque* might remind us of our high school struggles with another famous one that starts the great exordium ending in the assertive Ciceronian finger thrust at Catiline:

> *Quousque tandem abutere, Catilina, patientia nostra?*

If you want to teach the Latin language, you can use either sentence. Both have nouns and verbs. But if you want to form the sensibility — I will not say spirit, that would beg the question — but if in addition to teaching Latin you want to teach literature, if you want to have at the same time a culture, you cannot afford to neglect St. Bernard, any more than Cicero.

The third note of this monastic education is the agent cause: Who is the teacher? In a modern university very little attention is paid — or need be — to the teacher beyond his technical competence in the subject — not even his ability to teach and certainly not to his personal qualities, moral or spiritual. A judge in 1945 banned Bertrand Russell from teaching philosophy at City College in New York on the grounds that he advocated behavior that comes under the legal definition of statutory rape — Russell called it trial marriage. But today we say an expert is an expert and we want his expertise; what is it to us if the dentist confuses *Playboy* with literature so long as his fillings don't fall out, and it is the same with a philosopher. But if, like Socrates or St. Benedict, you say that there is something more than this, you have to pick your teacher and your textbooks with great care. In the long, raucous debate on censorship, each side has come to think the other is made up of lunatics and liars, largely because they have failed to distinguish the different uses of literature. If you take the modern view, reading rapidly for knowledge and delight, scholarship and criticism are for the establishing of texts and the classification of types and themes, and moral and spiritual evaluations are irrelevant, at best themselves subjects for classification. But if, in meditation, you take a text into your heart for the purpose of learning how to love, then Plato and the Christian tradition make sense. St. Benedict says of the teacher:

> Let him know what a difficult and arduous thing he undertakes — to regulate souls . . . for which he will one day render an account.

It isn't likely that a lecturer in chemistry or in the critical study of literature should ever be accused of corrupting youth, but anyone like Socrates or St. Benedict who undertakes the *regere animos* — the rule of souls — is open to the charge.

Plato said that all philosophy is a meditation on death. His own is certainly one long meditation on the death of Socrates — the whole Platonic corpus is a vast apology. The charge is not absurd, he says. Teachers are indeed responsible for what they teach, but Socrates is innocent. Socrates is the good teacher, a philosopher, a lover of wisdom, and therefore himself the just man of the Republic. St. Benedict's Abbot, in addition, must be the Just Man of the Scriptures, just like Socrates in the order of justice, justified by faith in the order of grace,

> fearing always the examination which the shepherd will have to face for the sheep entrusted to him; and, anxious regarding the account which will have to be given for others, he is made solicitous for his own sake also; and while by his admonitions helping others to amend, he himself is cleansed of his faults.

Anyone whose teaching crosses this line from the strict impersonality of science must always live precariously in a society managed by the politics of power and success, which is one of the reasons for the institution of protected sanctuaries such as colleges and convents under academic and clerical freedom, where the teacher is first subjected to rigorous ethical codes and a long initiation before receiving the rights of tenure — but once he has them, then is free from partisan interference.

But even granting this, Plato's final defense of Socrates is that really he is not the teacher anyway: the slave boy in the *Meno* learns the truth about the doubling of squares and incommensurables not from Socrates, who merely questions him, but from the interior magister who sits in the private conclave at the center of the soul and whom St. Augustine in the *De Magistro* identifies as the Logos of St. John.

Though monastic education is intensely personal, beginning with the mutual love and influence of student and teacher, it is nonetheless rigorously objective. It is not a Romantic personalism, not an emotional possession, but more like the psychoanalyst's who questions and listens but never intervenes, drawing out the patient's own personality so that he makes a self-discovery. Monastic education is not "transactional"; nothing is put in or exchanged. That would be to confuse love with a commodity, and its exercise with a technique. The teacher is not the author of the truth or even the agent of its discovery but an interlocutor and listener, an auxiliary, like the physician, who does not cause health but prudently assists nature to its own perfection.

The personal is not necessarily subjective, a distinction blurred by Romantics. The heart in classical and medieval symbolism is not the seat of the emotions but of the will — the intellectual appetite. Those today who fear Socratic and monastic methods most are often relativists who deny the existence of objective truth and therefore think such teaching must necessarily be some kind of hypnosis, failing to follow to the end the logic of their own position, which reduces all teaching to indoctrination, to behavior modification in varieties of conditioning, where reality itself, as the Buddhists say, is an illusion worked by a demonic hypnotist. No course of monastic studies can coerce the free intelligence which *sees* Intelligence and Love Himself, Who teaches from within. In the famous words of St. Augustine:

> *Sero te amavi, pulchritudo tam antiqua et tam nova, sero te amavi. Et ecce, intus eras, et ego foris!*

> Too late I loved thee, Beauty at once so ancient and so new, too late I loved thee. And behold, you were within and I without.

St. Teresa of Avila's *Interior Castle*, which is one of the two most widely read works in the Spanish language, according to Allison Peers, her translator, along with *Don Quixote* — a strange and marvelous team! — is a brightly colored print of this central fact about monastic education, in her case Carmelite. Written in 1577, looking back on the whole epoch, it is perhaps the best introduction to the Middle Ages there is. She begins,

> While I was beseeching Our Lord today that He would speak through me, since I could find nothing to say and had no idea how to begin to carry out the obligation laid upon me by obedience [i.e., the obligation of writing this book], a thought occurred to me which I will now set down in order to have some foundation on which to build. I began to think of the soul as if it were a castle made of a single diamond, or of very clear crystal, in which there are many rooms, just as in Heaven there are many mansions. Now if we think carefully over this, sisters, the soul of the righteous man is nothing but a paradise, in which, as God tells us, He takes His delight . . . But the senses and faculties [the inhabitants] have gone out of the castle, and for days and years, have been consorting with strangers, to whom all the good things in the castle are abhorrent. Then, realizing how much they have lost, they come back to it, though they do not actually re-enter it, because the habits they have formed are hard to conquer. But they are no longer traitors, and they now walk about in the vicinity of the castle. The great King Who dwells in the Mansion, within the castle, perceives their good will, and in His great mercy desires to bring them back to Him. So, like a good shepherd, with a call so gentle that even they can hardly recognize it, He teaches them to know His voice and not to go away and get lost but to return to their Mansion; and so powerful is this Shepherd's call that they give up the things outside the castle which had led them astray and once again enter it . . . But I cannot say where they entered it or how they heard their Shepherd's call: it was certainly not with their ears, for outwardly such a call is not audible. They become markedly conscious that they are gradually retiring within themselves; anyone who ex-

periences this will discover what I mean: I cannot explain it better. I think I have read that they are like a hedgehog or a tortoise withdrawing into itself . . .

The Bride in the Song of Songs says, "The King brought me" or "put me," I think the words are, "into the cellar of wine." It does not say that she *went*. It also says that she was wandering about in all directions seeking her Beloved. This, as I understand, is the cellar where the Lord is pleased to put us, *when* He wills and *as* He wills. But we cannot enter by any efforts of our own. His Majesty must put us right into the center of our soul, and must enter there Himself; and, in order that He may the better show us His wonders, it is His pleasure that our will, which has entirely surrendered itself to Him, should have no part in this. Nor does He desire the door of the faculties and senses, which are all asleep, to be opened to Him; He will come into the centre of the soul without using a door, as He did when He came in to His disciples, and said *Pax vobis*, and when He left the sepulcher without removing the stone.[17]

The fourth, last, note: the matter of monastic studies is eternal life. Lingering in all of us is a vague genetic memory of Paradise, where God conversed with Adam walking in the garden in the hours after noon; and some to whom this memory has a certain "presence," like Moses, Jacob, and especially David, are taken as figures of the contemplative life. But the first professional monk and abbot was Elijah on Mount Carmel, who sent his disciple out to watch a tiny cloud rising from the sea in the shape of a footprint of a man, as the first mysterious sign. On Mount Horeb, having fled the wrath of Jezebel, fed by an angel on mysterious food forty days and nights, Elijah hears, at last, the still, small voice — not the roaring spirit that moves mountains, not the spirit of the raging fire, but

sibilus aurae tenuis
a whistling of a gentle air.

---

[17]Trans. by Allison Peers, Image Books, Garden City, N.Y., 1961.

174

Monastic education is essentially static — quiet and still — a curriculum no longer running anywhere; a course but not a track. It does not move across any measurable distance but only somewhere in the trackless wastes of Egypt, or inside the *hortus conclusus* in some unnumbered house in the heart of a city and in the heart of someone in that house, as in the depths of a sealed well. Such an education does not submit easily to tests and measurements; it baffles registrars; one never graduates. It seems like a retreat, a vacation though not an indolence — it is a zealous leisure; careless of footnotes and bibliographies, its sources are within. One doesn't read the hundred books or even the book reviews. A single verse suffices for an hour or a year and one forgets the chapters and the numbers. In meditative reading, speed kills. Notes and outlines interrupt. The student is like the bee gathering honey from several flowers — stuffed with sweetness, he forgets which ones were which — or like the worm who pushes forward blindly in the dark and then, accustomed to the place and knowing nothing of it save that he is there, pulls up his lower half: "This is a point of view," he says. "And though another may be greater and more splendid, none could be more true or ever quite the same!" — and pushes on again.

> *Vermis sum non homo.*
> I am a worm not a man.

And the Lord called to Adam and said: Where art thou? *Ubi es?* The Lord called him. Poor man who thinks he seeks the truth, like St. Augustine, crying in his anguish, "Thee will I seek!"

> *Quaeram te, domine . . .*

While in Carmel, in the interior mansion or desert cell, the medieval student reads and reads and reads again,

> *Vocavitque Dominus Deus Adam et dixit ei: Ubi es?*

"Tu reliquisti me!" God says to Jeremiah: "Thou hast left me." And all through the long afternoons in the quiet, watching the little cloud rising from the sea in the shape of a footprint, listening in the interior silence for the whistling of a gentle air, reading and rereading,

175

tracing what seem like accidental patterns through words and numbers and themes in the concordance of one's memory, in the great wheels within the wheels, turning with the seasons and the hours, tides, and stars, the liturgical year moves about the fixed point of the turning wheel.

There can be no doubt about the importance and validity of medieval studies to Western civilization, and no doubt that an interior participation (insofar as that is possible to those not actually living a monastic life) is, while not the *only* door, the *inner* door to the deepest understanding of medieval studies. The only question left is just what place there is for such an education in the modern university. When St. Benedict came up to Rome at the end of the fifth century, the world was already too modern for him; he drew his foot back from the university steps before it touched the stone. Is it not true that monastic education, while proper to monasteries, is not in the ordinary way of learning? Is not the proper business of universities scientific research — which can be applied profitably to medieval studies as to anything else, whose purpose is knowledge in the strict sense — *scientia* — leaving the love of God to religious institutions outside the tax supports of a government dedicated to the separation of church and state?

Very briefly:

1) The Constitution of the United States does not forbid the love of God to any citizen no matter what his color, creed, or job — not even if he is a teacher! It does forbid establishment of sect. Even the strictest application to colleges demands only that no student be required to take a course of sectarian religious studies, to participate in prayers, or to believe — in a word, there must be varieties and alternatives at the student's discretion and a faculty that respects conscience. The Constitution does not establish atheism.

What would the Constitution have us do? Draw up an index of forbidden books? Conduct autos-da-fe? Forbid the love of poetry; say, "Edit texts but don't believe what the texts say?" And how will you police belief? Shall we submit to polygraphs? Interrogations of our students? Forced and forged confessions? Intimidations, curtailments of privilege, mysterious inequities in salary and sabbatical leaves? Wire-taps? Tapes?

To say that freedom of religion excludes the right to teach what you believe is a contradiction in terms. It is a bitter joke to think of a university as the last refuge of religious bigotry. I have used the term *medieval* and not *Catholic* because the words are not coterminous. I wish they were. But, on the one hand, there are many Catholics moving away from the monastic center of their Church in the name of an untried spirit they falsely identify with the Second Vatican Council; and, on the other hand, there are some outside the visible Church who very well may be part of an invisible monastic tradition. So there is no question here at all of a religious establishment but, quite the reverse, of an inquisitorial Liberalism ruthlessly exterminating everything that disagrees with it — in the name of freedom.

2) There is a problem of appropriateness, a danger of what the schoolmen call "singularity" — of standing out of place — in attempting to adapt such an education to the machinery of the scientific majority that demands tests, schedules, and the like. Certainly compromises must be made. In France, England, Ireland, Canada — nations I happen to know; there are others too, I'm sure — there are denominational colleges within the secular universities, with cloisters, chapels, bells, and religious habits, witnessing to a full monastic life right in the middle of the academic confusion. In many universities there are institutes, departments, programs, friendly alliances, and single professors pursuing such studies — in all of which there is nothing contrary to American tradition or "disestablishmentarianism," and we should look forward to a major breakthrough against religious prejudice in American education when a monastic college is established at a state university, meanwhile encouraging programs and courses of such studies. It is not as if one were to propose a program of advocative assassin studies or a rapists' or cannibals' workshop; and in the teeth of the current permissiveness, the slighted medievalist must be forgiven a certain smile. Anti-Catholicism is the anti-Semitism of the Liberals — an easily vincible ignorance, and beneath contempt.

There will always be difficulties. Andrew White was right — there is antipathy, though not contradiction, between science and religion. There have been times when one has almost wiped the other out, but in a nation founded on pluralism, I can't see how a medieval presence can be excluded. Students have the right to learn, and therefore the right to try these texts and methods on their own and not their enemy's grounds. Given such an opportunity, not at all compelled or pressured, some will hear that whistling of a gentle air and find

vocations to the life, frequently to their parents' misunderstanding —
as in the case of St. Thomas Aquinas himself, imprisoned in a tower
to prevent his joining the Dominicans and quoting, I imagine,
Matthew 10:37 as he was lowered in a basket by his sisters to escape.
And for everyone in this buzzing, brawling technological age, especially for those opposed to its spirit, there is value in having a witness
to silence. Even if contemptible to some, the very foolishness and
frailty of this witness deserve a place against the day when brash
science and hard money may themselves become poor refugees from
their own success and need the friendship of a few survivors who have
believed all along that this world is a dark, though very beautiful,
night.

At least for now, in this disputed continent, the scientific suprem-
acy might stand for less than unconditional surrender and accept a
truce, finding something beautiful if neither good nor true in what it
has despised. St. Benedict believed that life itself is a kind of truce:

> *Ideo nobis propter emendationem malorum hujus vitae, dies ad*
> *indutias relaxantur.*

> Thus it is that for the emendation of the evils of this life,
> our days are lengthened for us by a truce.

Index

DATE DUE